The Four Wheels

The Four Wheels
Your Road Trip to Getting Real

Lisa A. Hendrickson

LitOne Publishing
Chicago

All anecodotes, references, and situations shared in this book are intended for illustration only only and do not refer to any specific person, company, or situation.

**THE FOUR WHEELS:
YOUR ROAD TRIP TO GETTING REAL**

Copyright 2024 by Lisa A. Hendrickson. No part of this work may be reproduced, scanned, or distributed in any way, including in print or electronic form, without the written permission of the publisher. All rights reserved.

Published by LitOne Publishing
4000 W Montrose Ave
Chicago IL 60641

www.litonepublishing.com | +1 312 620 2700

Book interior and cover design by LitOne Publishing. The Four Wheels logo is copyright Lisa A. Hendrickson. All other images used within this book source from the public domain.

ISBN-13:   978-1-943548-04-0 (softcover)
              978-1-943548-05-7 (ebook)

First Edition: July 2024
First Printing: July 2024

Printed in the United States of America.

Contents

Acknowledgements 1

1: Me 4
2: You 9
3: Bringing Others With You 14
4: Belief 24
5: Passion 53
6: Skill 69
7: Will 79
8: Put the Four Wheels in Motion 101
9: Hit the Road 122

The Four Wheels Tool Box 129

Cheers to My Ride-or-Dies
For My Travel Companions

As with every adventure, it's the people you bring along with you that make all the difference. I'm lucky to have these ride-or-dies in my corner, as a woman and as a writer. I would not be the person I am today or have had the courage to finish this book without you. I am forever grateful to call you mine.

To my parents. You instilled in me the belief that I could do and be anything, and that taking chances often changes life for the better. It's a confidence I carry with me every day. Your core values are the guiding light in my life: *Be kind to others. Treat them as you want to be treated. Seek the best in yourself. Be a powerful force for good in this world.* You are my most ardent supporters and prayer warriors.

To Todd. I did it! It's been one wild ride and you've been with me through it all. I look forward to our next chapter.

To Aaron. You and I have a bond like none other. Once, it was you and me against the world. You are forever first to reach out with love on a special day and first to offer your help when I need you. Love you to the moon and back.

To Austin. You are a kind, sensitive and giving soul. You lift me up daily with your humor, compassion and love. Watching you grow into a wonderful young man inspires me. Love you more.

To Jayden. You sprinkle a bit of girl power in our home. For all your glitter and grace, you are one of the best surprises of my life.

To Susan. Thank you for being my constant cheerleader. Our differences make our connection stronger, and we come together in our love and respect for one another. You are one of the smartest and most intuitive people I know, and our friendship has dramatically changed my life for the better. Without your belief in me, this book wouldn't have happened.

To Tom. Many years ago, while I was working on yet another family vacation, you gave me a nugget of wisdom: "The only person who should benefit from your work ethic is you." It took me some time to "get" your sage advice, but it finally sunk in. And it's made all the difference.

To Teri. No matter how much time passes or where we are in our journeys, I can always count on the fact that we've got each other's backs. And that has made all the difference.

To Jean. I learned so much from you about the power of influence, advocating for others and being poised in front of the camera.

To Tracy. Your fearlessness and belief in

possibilities inspires me. You pushed our team to be better and think differently and it made all the difference to me.

To Dr. Reuben and Sunny. From traveling the world together to learning the nuances of a global successful family owned business, I appreciate our partnership very much.

To Sandy. Thank you for being a trail blazer and my friend. Our connection has taken me to some of the best stops on my journey.

To Anton. Who knew that a chance introduction could turn into one of the most amazing journeys ever?

To Carol. As one of my newer "wingwomen" you are a force and a great support!

To all the friends I've made through my coaching. Thank you for showing up and showing me who you are. By welcoming me into your lives, I have learned and grown in immeasurable ways in my own life. I hold your stories, your families, and your successes in my heart, always.

Chapter 1
Me

While it feels indulgent to start this journey by shining the spotlight on yours truly, it's important that I earn your respect. So please indulge me, only for a moment, so we can get to what really matters: you.

Coach, trainer, speaker, strategist, entrepreneur, C-suite exec—needless to say, I have played many roles in my career, some starring, some supporting, always interesting. Along the way, I have been integral in creating training and development programs that have been foundational to the growth of non-profit organizations, Fortune 500 companies, and global direct sellers. I'm a forward thinker, unafraid to challenge companies and executives to grow and pivot, in order to stay ahead of the curve.

I feel blessed to have guided and championed thousands of sales teams and business owners to achieve their goals, realize their true calling, and change the trajectory of their lives.

Simply put: I *love* what I do and I *love* the relationships and partnerships I have fostered over the years. Yet this love for my work has been all-consuming. While showing others the road to success, I have twisted and shaped most of my life around their needs and wants while my own have taken a backseat. Why, you ask?

Because I am a perfectionist. I hold myself to the highest standards and don't like making mistakes. It's a blessing and a curse. One of my earliest memories is writing a paper in elementary school and rewriting it several times because the penmanship wasn't perfect.

I am an overachiever. I work hard and give my all in everything I do—even if that means working seven days a week, 12 or more hours a day.

I am tenacious and have made a career on being upwardly mobile. Executives know they can count on me to get the job done and I have been rewarded for that work ethic. Even in my first "real job" as a file clerk, I moved into upper management in record time and kept going, up and up and up until I reached the proverbial ceiling.

I am a contributor. Giving back is my go-to and paramount to me.

Above all, I am a servant leader. My love for

people makes their well-being my priority. And helping them realize their highest potential is truly my privilege. It's what gets me out of bed in the morning, my driving force, my life's calling. And I am good at it. I have helped dozens of companies achieve record, game-changing growth. I have inspired thousands of business owners do what they never thought possible.

I'm lucky to love what I do but it's been life-changing work that's taken a significant toll on my life. A few years ago, I found myself at a crossroads, overwhelmed and under the weight of my own success. As I reflected on the things that I had always lauded as my strengths, it dawned upon me that these attributes had perpetuated a lifestyle that had become less than desirable.

In my personal life, no matter how much I had on my plate, no matter how mighty the ask, I was known as the go-to person for just about everyone. I remember teasing my family that I felt like Lucy in the *Peanuts* comics giving out 5¢ therapy or an ATM spitting out cash or the DIY expert who could fix just about anything. Suffice it to say, I was exhausted.

Work was no different. I put the needs of the company before my and my family's needs. I was the first to show up and the last to leave. I rarely took vacations and made myself available to my bosses and teams around the clock.

I knew that I needed to make a change and put my money where my mouth was. More on that later.

As diverse as my career has been, the common thread throughout my years of coaching, over thousands of conversations, was crystal clear to me: People at a crossroads in life and at work are inherently bound by four simple yet profound truths: belief, passion, skill, will.

Why do individuals that once had goals or dreams that burned like a fire within them suddenly find themselves struggling to put one foot in front of the other to make anything happen? Over time, some seemed to lose belief, in themselves and in their ability to even accomplish their goal at all. Some lost their passion, spark, or excitement for what drove them to want to set their goal in the first place. For others, at some point in the process of trying to meet their goal, they no longer felt equipped with the tools or talents they needed to be successful. Some even seemed to be hit by a curveball that derailed their very will to take the next step toward their success.

No matter the why, the how always came back to these four truths:

These four truths became the roadmap for my overall coaching strategy. I quickly discovered that, when I coached people to visualize Belief, Passion, Skill, and Will as the four wheels on the SUV they were taking on their journey, it became very easy to understand how losing one wheel, or even just being out of alignment, can greatly impact how they got from point A to point B—and even keep them from reaching their destination at all.

Simple yet profound, these Four Wheels inspired this book. Writing it has been a labor of love that answers the call of many people I've coached over the years who nudged me to share my "nuggets of wisdom" in one place.

This book is for you.

Chapter 2
You

If you are reading this book, you want something more for yourself.

Like I was, you may be feeling overwhelmed and at a crossroads in your life. Perhaps the things you have been chasing most of your life and may have attained after much hustle, heart and sacrifice, are not really doing it for you like you thought they would. Sometimes getting what you want—a bigger title, more money, higher status—isn't really what you need, is it?

Maybe those whose vision you have supported, championed, and aligned yourself with suddenly look differently to you—and not a *good* different. Why has life seemingly lost its luster?

Or maybe you have spent much of your life climbing the mountain, going back to base camp and climbing again, only to find that when you finally made it to the summit, the fog set in. Why does everything feel hazy?

Perhaps the personal sacrifices you have made over many years of supporting the vision of others to get your "dream job" (or dream of any kind) now feel more significant than the achievements themselves?

Are you too exhausted, overwhelmed, or even paralyzed to take the step you need to change direction and get to a different place in your life? Over the years, little by little, have you lost pieces of yourself to others? And as time went on, have you become almost unrecognizable to yourself?

Trust me, I get it. And I promise you: The happy, confident, optimistic, capable, agile, fearless, successful someone you were destined to be is still in there.

You might even be thinking: *How did I get here? Where along the way did I lose myself? When did I start allowing others to define my value and self-worth?*

Today you may be unhappy, unconfident, negative, even afraid. Know that I have been where you are. And if you too feel scared of everything, especially failure, rest assured that you *can* change. And your life will be better for it.

Dig deep. You know that this shift in who

you are versus who you want to be hasn't been overnight. This process took time. It happened over years of personal and professional sacrifice. Of putting the needs, desires, and demands of others before your own. Of giving them more power than they deserved. Of allowing them to steal your joy and measure your worth.

Today is also the day to begin to put one foot in front of the other and forge a new path with new goals. It's time to get what you deserve. It's time to put your wheels in motion.

You can do it because *you* are worth it. Say it out loud, "I am worth it!"

Congratulations, you've just declared you're ready to get started.

Before you begin any journey, you want to make sure that you pack the right stuff. We've all been on a trip where we wished we packed something that we left behind and found ourselves distracted by all of the amazing things we saw by dwelling on the "what if I only had this". Let's eliminate that distraction now. On your Four Wheels journey, there are three important tools to pack. Take time to read and complete them because you will need them before you dive into the next chapter.

The Right Stuff

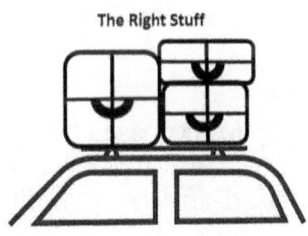

Distraction, Be Gone

The speed of life is ever increasing. As our pace quickens, so does our level of distraction.

In order to be fully open to any new concept, you must understand the distractions that you will encounter and master how to overcome them to get the results you want. The success of your journey depends on it.

You may get distracted by friends and family who don't share your excitement and try to derail you.

You may get distracted if you don't fully agree with a particular concept or doubt that it will work.

You may get distracted if you have multiple voices in your head. Fully embracing your journey is difficult if you have too many people pointing you in too many directions.

You may get distracted if you are tired or uncomfortable or are under personal stress.

Remember that while distraction is a given on any journey, *you are in control*. When you feel distraction creeping in, take a deep breath and make the conscious decision to push through and refocus your eyes on the prize. The choice is yours.

SWOT Up

Strengths. Weaknesses. Opportunities. Threats. Do you know yours? Doing a SWOT analysis is a tried-and-true method and best practice in business to identify internal strengths and weaknesses and external opportunities and threats. This assessment guides successful business and marketing plans by providing critical information for creating strategic plans for growth. Your life is no different.

With this in mind, you will complete a personal SWOT, which you can find in The Four Wheels Tool Box in the appendix of this book. Like a roadmap, this creative self-assessment tool will help you better navigate how to play to your own strengths and manage your own weaknesses, as well as uncover opportunities for growth and eliminate threats that could keep you from moving forward on your journey.

Oh Joy, Journal

There's power in writing things down. Daily journaling helps you capture your feelings, epiphanies, areas of opportunity, goals, and more as you make your way.

Set yourself up for success by setting aside 10 to 15 minutes each day for journaling. Any time of day works, so choose what's best for you. And don't be shy–the more real you are, the more likely your success.

Chapter 3
Your GPS

Any adventure is a whole lot more fun if you bring others along on your journey.

Better yet, bring those who believe in you.

After all, no one needs a backseat driver telling them where they should and shouldn't be going or that they are driving too fast or too slow or that if they were driving, they would have turned here or turned there.

You need a navigator who knows where YOU want to go, a trusted confidante who will help keep you focused so you don't get lost along the way. No time for detours on the way to your destination.

Your navigator will not only help to keep you on track, but also help you honor the commitment you made to start the journey in the first place. They will help keep you motivated and give you advice when asked. They will help you push through the rainstorms, get around the potholes and celebrate the days when you reach milestone points on your destination map.

Choosing the right navigator is important in the success of your journey. If you choose someone who is destination challenged themselves, they may not be able to help you stay on course or hold you accountable.

What makes a great navigator? Consider these points:

- They are not a family member. (Navigators must be neutral.)
- They understand you and what you are trying to accomplish.
- They care about you.
- They are trustworthy.
- They are dependable, so you can call on them when needed.
- They have accomplished some level of success in their own life or business.
- They are non-judgmental. They remain

objective in their opinions and experience life from an "it is what it is" view.
- They can lift you up with a pep talk or tell it like it is when you ask for their honest advice.
- They are positive and see the rainbows in the storms.

The Big Ask

Once you have your navigator in mind, don't overthink asking for their support. It's as simple as sharing these words:

"I am working toward a goal that will make a big difference in (my life, my family, or my career). Part of my journey toward this goal is choosing a navigator to help keep me on track. I thought of you first because (share why you chose them—choose one or two of the characteristics on the previous page). Can I count on you?"

If your navigator is the right person, they will probably ask questions like these. Here's how you can respond:

What does keeping you on track look like?

"To keep me on track, we need to agree upon how I would like to be held accountable to my goal. The help determine this, the question I would like you to ask me is: I am so excited to help you get (your goal) this month! I care enough about you and your goal to hold you accountable to it. If there ever becomes a time where I see you are struggling to reach this goal, or your words are not meeting your actions, how would you like me to handle that?

"This will help me be in charge of setting the expectation, so that you simply have to hold me to it."

How much time will you need from me?

"It's as simple as a scheduled check-in. Would a (weekly, bi-weekly) check-in for 15 minutes work for you?"

Sharing Your Why

After your navigator is onboard, be sure to share your goal and the driving force behind it. This is your *why*, and you must know it before you contact your navigator.

Sharing your why with your navigator should sound something like this:

"My goal is ...."

"It is important to me because ...."

"When I achieve my goal I will feel ...."

"When I achieve my goal, I think my family will feel ...."

It is important that your navigator fully understand the importance of your why and your emotion behind achieving your goal. Without this information, your navigator will find it more difficult to keep you on track.

Equally important to having a navigator on your journey is having your family or loved ones support your goals. Consider them the spare tire in your journey.

Throughout my coaching of entrepreneurs,

I have framed this support of your family as your Board of Directors. You're the CEO of your life and, like most successful CEOs, you need a Board of Directors who:

- Looks out for "*shareholders*'" interests
- Weighs in on strategic decisions
- Supports the strategic vision
- Helps to act in crisis situations

It is inevitable that life will get in the way. You will run into a pothole or get a flat tire. When this happens, it's helpful when the people who are closest to you are rallying behind you. And if they're not, then they are either complacent or rallying against you—neither is helpful to you as you drive your goals.

If your Board of Directors isn't "on board" with your goals, you will be fighting battles behind the scenes that will derail your success. So it's important to bring the people you care most about into the family boardroom to come up with shared goals and regular check ins. When you do, everyone has a stake in the final destination.

Scheduling a monthly family board meeting creates a unified vision and provides purpose to your family organization.

When the goals are met, everyone benefits

in some way and peace is kept in the family because everyone gets what they want.

Meet Wendy

Wendy was an independent business owner who came to me for coaching because it was total chaos at home. She was frustrated, anxious, and, quite frankly, over her entire family.

Matt and Wendy had been married for 17 years. Their 15-year-old son, Josh, was struggling in school and their 12-year-old daughter, Erin, had made back-talking an art form by constantly arguing with their 7-year-old daughter, Morgan, who was starting to adopt the behaviors of her siblings.

Matt was never home, and when he was, he disconnected from the family by watching sports on TV and wanting to be left alone.

Wendy's early entrepreneurial success had started to decline, and she was at a make-or-break point with whether to keep going in her business.

After speaking with Wendy at length, I found out that Matt was working two jobs to pay off major debt in hospital bills from an illness that Morgan had a couple of years prior. The hospital sent the family to collections and Matt was upset because he valued their perfect credit. While Wendy started her business to help with the medical debt and had some quick success, it wasn't enough to really make a dent in their bills and keep Matt from working two jobs.

Before Morgan's illness, their family life was completely different. They were involved in their church and in family and school activities. Although Morgan had fully recovered, their family life had not. Over the two years of Morgan's illness, they had stopped attending church and had limited time for activities. There just weren't enough hours in the week between caring for Morgan and working the extra jobs.

While they did have a bit more time in their schedule with Morgan's recovery, things were so far off the rails that Wendy didn't know how to get it all back on track.

It was obvious to me that everyone in Wendy's household was either paralyzed, stressed out, or tired. Matt working two jobs had him coming home at night and wanting to be left alone. While it was upsetting to Wendy and the kids, he needed the downtime to disconnect. Morgan's recovery hadn't really changed his schedule. Although Matt had taken time off for Morgan's big appointments and procedures, he was still working seven days a week, with five days spent juggling two jobs. Easily irritated, his naturally upbeat personality had drastically changed.

Josh was tired of his dad not being around. Josh and Matt at one time had been almost inseparable. They hung out together and Matt attended every one of Josh's sporting events he could. Erin was tired of not getting Wendy's attention. They too had been inseparable prior to Morgan's illness. Erin was jealous of Morgan and anything Morgan said or did set Erin off. Morgan was starting to lash out at everyone, and even her grades were slipping.

Wendy and I discussed how they could make a couple of small steps to get everyone back on track.

We talked about having a family board meeting (*see examples in The Four Wheels Tool Box, in the appendix*) and allowing everyone to both clear the air and set some family goals to get everyone working together. Wendy agreed to get everyone together on Friday night over pizza since Matt was off work that night.

Saturday morning, I received the following email from Wendy:

Hi Lisa,
First, I want to thank you for pushing me to hold this family meeting. I know that I had a whole lot of fear about it because things have been so ugly for so many months.

I really thought that Matt would fight it but he was so open to the meeting and making a change. The kids too. I think we had all had it.

You asked me to take notes and send them next week, but I am so excited about how the meeting went

that I wanted to send the notes right away.
Good News:
No one had anything to share at first, but I really pressed them to share something, anything. Here's what they each said:
Matt: If this meeting helps then that's good news for me.
Josh: I didn't fail my chemistry test this week.
Erin: Sari told me that she liked my outfit.
Morgan: Megan shared the cookies her grandma made at lunch with me.
Wendy: The fact that you aren't fighting me on this meeting is good news.
Set goals: What is the big goal?
To get Dad home more.
The kids will help more so that mom will have more time to work her business to get Dad home.
Define Roles and Responsibilities: Who is doing what?
Dad: Is going to spend less time in front of the TV and more time doing things with the family.
Josh: In addition to his chores he is going to add keeping up with his homework and helping mom with social media on Saturday mornings.
Erin: In addition to her chores she is going to add making dinner two nights a week so mom has more time to earn more money in her business.
Morgan: In addition to her chores she is going to add helping with the laundry.
Wendy: Is going to fully work her business two nights a week to earn more.

Define Rewards: What's in it for each of us?

All: When mom is earning $400 more a month, she can take over some of the hospital bills so that Dad won't have to work as many nights on his other job.

Then we can all start doing family night things and Dad and can spend more time with us.

Inspirational Close:

Morgan said a prayer and we all put our hands in for a family huddle.

We ended the meeting with pizza and watched a movie together for the first time in almost two years.

I am in tears. Thank you!

Hugs,
Wendy

When you bring others along on your journey who support you, hold you accountable and get you back on track, you have a spare tire that can save the day when one of your regular wheels calls it quits.

Chapter 4

Belief is your destination.

Belief is such a powerful concept that, when you truly understand how powerful it is, it can change your life.

When we are full of belief, we see endless possibilities. When we are short on belief, we see only limitations.

Belief can instill comfort and confidence, purpose and connection. Belief ignites our passion, fuels our confidence to persevere and gives us strength of will.

Think about belief as a three-step process:
1. Your beliefs determine your actions.
2. Your actions determine your results.

3. Your results reinforce your beliefs.

What this means is that belief is shaped by our experiences and is the foundation for our purpose and our commitments.

The beliefs that you hold to be true are based upon a lifetime of experiences. The stronger the experience to support the belief, the stronger the belief and the more you will find reasons to support it.

For most of us, our strongest beliefs are not really true. Rather, we have rationalized them to become true to us over time. Simply put: Our experiences have helped us decide that our beliefs are fact. Whether we have done this consciously or unconsciously, it makes no difference.

Beliefs are formed through thoughts that are reaffirmed over and over throughout your lifetime. And the only reason that they carry the weight that they do is because you have consciously or unconsciously decided or agreed that your beliefs are true to *you*.

For example, using the three-step process of belief, you might say:

"My friends are so busy today, that's why no one wants to do a girls' night out after work. When I call them to ask, I am just bothering them. If they really wanted to hang out after work, they would call or text me."

Your belief is that your friends are so busy that they really do not want to hang out after work and, if you call or text them, you will be bothering them. If they really wanted to hang out, they would reach out to you.

Based upon your belief, your action is that you don't pick up the phone. You don't text. You don't ask your friends to hang out after work.

Because your action is to not reach out to your friends, your result is no happy hour after work. This result then reinforces your belief to say; "See, I am right! No one wants to hang out after work!"

You can see how limiting this can be over time, right?

But what if you changed the process and, rather than start with your belief, you started with the opposite action? The one that is *not* based on your belief?

For example: Despite your belief that your friends are too busy to hang out after work and, if you reach out to them, you are bothering them, you do it anyway. Instead of taking the action to refrain from calling or texting, you actually suck it up and call or text.

Because your action now is to reach out to your friends, you will probably have one or two take you up on your offer, which changes your result!

Your new result is the first step in chipping away at the old belief.

Limiting beliefs are dangerous because they become so ingrained in us over time, that it's easier to live with them than to eliminate them. Or worse yet, we don't even realize we have limiting beliefs until someone calls us out.

There are a whole lot of collective limiting beliefs that you have probably talked yourself into over the course of your lifetime. Do any of these sound familiar?

- It's just the way I was raised
- I am too old
- I am not tech savvy
- I am not that smart
- I have the worst luck
- I am a klutz
- I always choose the wrong men/women
- I always make the wrong decisions
- Dreams are for the young
- I don't deserve it

Conversely, there are also some limiting beliefs that you have personally acquired through your unique experiences. Most of these types of beliefs were adopted unconsciously because you lived the experience and the belief stuck.

None of us sets out to hold onto beliefs that limit us and keep us from achieving the things that we want in life. Nevertheless, beliefs are like noodles on the wall: Over time, some stick to us and are difficult to remove.

And the more time that passes, the easier it is to rationalize limiting beliefs by telling ourselves things like: "this is the way I am" (it's too hard to change now) or "this is the way things are" (others agree with me).

Personal beliefs like "this is the way I am" have often become such a large part of our identity that we have created habits and patterns to support them.

Collective beliefs like "this is the way things are" can also be difficult to eliminate because we have gravitated toward others who think like we do to give our beliefs credibility—we feel the commonality proves that we are right.

If we don't make an effort to move past our limiting beliefs, they become giant potholes that are obstacles in getting to our destination. And just like potholes, limiting beliefs take a bit of time and effort to repave. But once we fix them, we will be driving on a beautiful newly paved stretch of our journey.

So how do you move past limiting beliefs? There are several things we can do to move past limiting beliefs so that we can get to our destination.

Stop letting the belief define you.

If you tell yourself that you are not tech savvy, you are rationalizing your belief through procrastination (more about this later in the book). When you procrastinate, you find any possible way to avoid doing something that you don't want to do. Procrastination is often driven by fear. So, while it might be really scary to step out of your comfort zone and tackle new tech skills like setting up a website or social media platform, you must push past your fear and be okay with taking baby steps and stumbling a bit along the way.

Stop agreeing with the masses.

Don't be a follower–you're a free thinker! While

it might make you feel right and righteous to agree with the collective group, if the belief is limiting your progress you must boldly break away from the pack. Just because everyone else thinks that the new website is difficult to use, doesn't mean you don't have to embrace the change. Step out of your comfort zone and do what you can to lean in and learn to move forward.

Retrain your brain.

Put your brain in boot camp. There is an old adage that says, "My brain is not as smart as I think it is." What this means is that your brain will believe anything you tell it, if you tell it often enough. If you go through your life telling yourself that you aren't tech savvy, you will never be tech savvy. If you go through your life telling yourself that you always make the wrong decisions, you will always make poor choices. Instead, flip the script and turn your limiting belief to the positive. Take your brain from, "I am not tech savvy" to "I *am* tech savvy."

Give yourself permission to push boundaries.

Use the three-step process of belief to push past your assumptions and conclusions in order to create a new belief.

Strengthen your belief system.

Give your beliefs a work-out. Ultimately, you are in the driver's seat with your beliefs. You decide what you tell yourself every day. Infuse yourself with new ideas and beliefs through reading. You never want to be the smartest person in the room—surround yourself with others who exemplify your new belief.

Positive affirmations are another way to strengthen your belief and retrain your brain. While you may think they are overused, they truly work! Positivity is a superpower.

Meet Hannah

Hannah came to me because her business was stagnant. She needed to grow her income, and she needed to do it quickly. She felt stuck and needed fresh business ideas. The things that were working for others in their businesses just weren't working for her.

After speaking with Hannah at length, it became clear that her sense of urgency was due to the strained relationship with her husband, Ryan. Her marriage was struggling because Ryan expected her business to have become more successful more quickly than it had. Hannah had been in business for a year and Ryan wasn't seeing the positive impact that she promised in their home life. In his words, Ryan felt he "had been picking up the slack at home and was over it." Ryan issued an ultimatum: Hannah had 60 days to make more income to help support the family or she needed to give up her business.

Meet Grace

Grace reached out to me because she was struggling at work. While she loved her job, her boss, Lauren, was making her work and home life undesirable. Lauren was self-absorbed, mistrusting, passive aggressive, and reactive. Lauren fed on drama and gravitated toward and elevated those in the organization who were toxic and difficult to work with. Lauren's boundaries frequently overstepped traditional working hours, well into the late evening and early morning. While Lauren frequently shared that she did not expect an immediate after hour response from her team, she would react harshly and make rash decisions that derailed the success of projects when her team did not respond immediately.

Grace frequently received these snide emails from Lauren and was up all night reading between the lines. Lauren's behavior caused Grace to become paranoid, insecure, and unconfident. This chaos was causing issues at home. Grace's husband, John, wanted her to confront Lauren head-on, but Grace knew that Lauren's personality would not tolerate this behavior. There were even times where Lauren could be complimentary and generous, which caused Grace to second-guess leaving or confronting Lauren. Grace knew this was not a healthy work environment, yet she felt paralyzed to make a change and needed outside help.

Hannah

There were a couple of things that jumped out at me after I reflected on my conversation with Hannah. Hannah said that she was "stuck" and needed "fresh ideas." The things that were working for others "just weren't working for her." The pressure that Ryan was putting on Hannah wasn't helping either.

Hannah started a business to help her family. When things didn't click for her the way that she anticipated, she began to compare herself to others in the business who were rock stars. It didn't matter that she didn't really know these people or the challenges they may have encountered or the time it may have taken them to kick things into gear. Hannah couldn't understand why doing what they were doing didn't give her the same results. When Ryan began to put pressure on Hannah, she felt desperate and panicked. Her belief in her ability to succeed eroded.

Grace

After speaking with Grace, it was obvious that she was in a toxic situation and needed a change of environment. Her situation was affecting her work life, her confidence, and her family life. The caveat here is that, often when people are in a terrible environment like this, they will jump too quickly at the first opportunity—and often, the first opportunity is not the best.

John wanted Grace to confront Lauren head on because John was feeling helpless for his wife. He saw the changes in Grace and simply wanted to fix the situation. But this wasn't an easy fix. A personality like Lauren does not see the error of their ways and is not open to confrontation. Grace needed help managing her current work environment, as well as help in getting John to see that she was navigating things well. Only then would Grace begin to feel more confident, less paralyzed and more open to making a career move.

Hannah

Hannah needed a belief boost. She also needed to understand why she was stuck. I asked her to complete the Belief Grid (Appendix — The Four Wheels Tool Box).

These were her responses, in italics:

Think of a time when you should have taken a step but didn't—a time when you really wanted to put something into action but fell short.

In childhood:
I can think of a couple. I always wanted to be on the school volleyball team, but I was too afraid to try out. I think I could have been good, because my

family always played volleyball at family picnics, and I was always the best player. I just wasn't a "trained" volleyball player so I wasn't sure if being good at our family events would be good enough to make the team.

In grade school, there was a girl at our school who was an outsider. She was a little quirky but smart and nice. The other kids really made fun of her for stupid reasons. They didn't like the way she wore her hair or dressed. Things like that. Secretly I liked her because she always had the answers and I liked that she didn't seem to care what everyone thought. But it has always bothered me because I bet, deep down, she was hurt and I never took a step to reach out to her.

In adult life:
I kind of go along. I never want to make waves even when I really want to because I think that people are being mean or stupid.

What stopped you from taking the step?

In childhood:
I was afraid to fail or be the outsider myself.

In adult life:
Like I said before, I don't like to make waves.

What holds me back from achieving what it is I want? What are the barriers in my way?
Ryan is very successful and has strong opinions

on things. *Sometimes I feel lost when I am in the room with him. If I start to fail at anything I just want to quit.*

Why am I here?
I want my business to be successful because I want to contribute and be proud of my contributions.

In thinking of my life today, what is it that I want more of?
More confidence and assertiveness. I think if I was more assertive, I would have reached out to others more.

If I knew I could not fail, and all barriers were removed, what would my life or business look like?

This month?
I would be making our car payment of $412 per month.

This year?
I would have our car paid off at the end of this year.

In five years?
I would be working my business on my terms and be able to do more for my family.

What limiting beliefs do I tell myself? (In all aspects of my life – business and personal):
I am not assertive.
I am not a risk taker.

I am not as good as the other people in the business.
I am not good enough.
I am not creative.
I am a quitter.

Do I use daily positive affirmations? Why or why not?
No, it feels weird.

If I could change one thing tomorrow, what would it be?
I would like to be more successful.

Do I believe I am someone who is worthy and who can have all they want in life? Why or why not?
No. Maybe if I had some success I might.

Reviewing Hannah's responses to the Belief Grid made it clear that her fear of failure had been holding her back from the success that she desired. Because she was afraid to fail, she was paralyzed from the action she needed to see a change in her life.

For example, if she had joined the volleyball team, she would have received coaching to be successful which would have changed her perspective. Fear of failure made Hannah so insecure that, if she suffered even the smallest misstep, she would project failure and quit. In quitting, Hannah stopped the failure before it happened. This same fear of failure affected

Hannah's relationships with others. She lived in her husband's shadow and had become a follower rather than a leader. This caused her to feel inferior to others.

Hannah needed to retrain her brain and have a couple of small wins, so that she could begin to see her value and worth.

After speaking with Hannah, we decided on the following course of action:

Choose one limiting belief that she would tackle over the next 21 days and retrain her brain. Hannah chose "I am a quitter." Over the next 21 days, Hannah would retrain her brain through daily affirmations to support this changing perspective.

In addition to the daily affirmations, Hannah would choose one act of motion that she had abandoned or ignored because she was afraid of failing. Hannah would go full-court-press on this act of motion for 21 days. We focused on Hannah's original conversation to help us with her act of motion.

Hannah said that she was "stuck" and needed "fresh ideas." The things that were working for others "just weren't working for her."

When pressed, Hannah admitted that she really hadn't given the company training a chance. Rather than actually attending the trainings, she cherry picked the ideas she liked from others who had taken the trainings. After some coaching, Hannah began to understand that, taking only parts of the training rather than the training as a whole, could have impeded her success. Over the next 21 days, Hannah agreed to start the company training program in order and complete the activities as they were presented.

We also discussed Ryan's ultimatum. I asked Hannah to consider Ryan's responses over the past few months. Was there a possibility that Ryan issued his ultimatum because he wasn't seeing the acts of motion in the business? Could issuing the ultimatum be Ryan's way of lighting a fire under Hannah?

I shared the Board of Directors framework with Hannah (Appendix – The Four Wheels Tool Box) and asked her to schedule a meeting with Ryan to clear the air and set some shared goals.

Three weeks later, Hannah and I met for a progress report. She shared that putting her brain through boot camp was tough. For the first few days, she found herself slipping back into her fear of failure routine but, as days went on, she felt more and more confident. The company training was making a difference and she was feeling more confident about her business.

She and Ryan had their Board of Directors meeting and worked together on setting shared goals. Clearing the air helped Ryan understand Hannah's deeply rooted fear of failure and they locked arms for their family.

Six months later, Hannah reported positive change in both her business and her relationship with Ryan. While she continued to have moments where she felt unconfident or insecure, she continued with the daily affirmations and even began to tackle more limiting beliefs. Hannah also shared that she felt less in Ryan's shadow and more like a leader herself.

Grace

In order to help Grace navigate her current work environment and alleviate some of the paralysis that she was feeling, I asked her to complete the Belief Grid (Chapter 8).

These were her responses, in italics:

Think of a time when you should have taken a step but didn't—a time when you really wanted to put something into action but fell short.

In childhood:
There was a very popular girl in high school who was the leader of a group of girls that everyone wanted to be friends with. I really, really wanted to be in this group. So when they asked me to hang out with them, it was like a dream come true. I joined the group and realized that not only were these girls popular, but they were also very mean. They did some really horrible things to other girls in high school and I just went along. Although I never did anything mean myself, I didn't defend anyone or leave the group. I am sure that there are girls who hate me to this day because of the things the group did.

In adult life:
I want to stop responding to Lauren after hours but I worry that I will upset her and lose my job.

What stopped you from taking the step?

In childhood:
I wanted to be popular and, because I wasn't actually being mean to others myself, I convinced myself that it was okay.

In adult life:
I don't want to lose my job.

What holds me back from achieving what it is I want? What are the barriers in my way?

I want others to like me, and I especially want Lauren to like me and appreciate me.

Why am I here?

I like my job and hope that Lauren someday gets another job, so I can stay.

In thinking of my life today, what is it that I want more of?

More control of my life.

If I knew I could not fail, and all barriers were removed, what would my life or business look like?

This month?
I wouldn't be working round the clock.

This year?
More control of my life.

In five years?
I would have my dream job and be happy.

What limiting beliefs do I tell myself? (In all aspects of my life – business and personal):
I am not worthy.
I don't have what it takes.
I am not strong enough.
I am too tired.
I am not good enough.

Do I use daily positive affirmations? Why or why not?
No, never thought about it.

If I could change one thing tomorrow, what would it be?
Lauren would be elsewhere, or I would be.

Do I believe I am someone who is worthy and who can have all they want in life? Why or why not?
I do believe that I can have more, but I am so exhausted that it seems a tall order sometimes.

We knew that Grace was in a toxic situation and needed a change of environment. But after reading Grace's responses, it was obvious that Grace had an extreme need to be liked by others.

Grace also needed others to validate her worth by showing their gratitude and appreciation—and she was a people pleaser. These character traits were so deeply ingrained in Grace from an early age that they would take some real re-training. As for her relationship with Lauren, I knew that we couldn't change Lauren's behavior, but I could help to Grace to change her reaction to Lauren and her overall perspective on her role in the company.

The first thing we discussed was allowing Lauren to put her money where her mouth was. Remember that Grace shared that Lauren said she did not expect an immediate after hour's response from her team.

When I challenged Grace about this, she expressed her fear of the consequences in not responding to Lauren's every whim.

"Okay," I responded, "let's make a list of all the consequences that could happen if you don't respond to Lauren after hours."

Grace immediately started lobbing consequences"

"She might get angry with me.

"If she is angry, she will be passive aggressive and send me snarky emails or texts.

"She might execute an idea that would conflict with something we already have in the works.

"She might fire me.

"She might put me on her list and be rude and condescending to me until she decides she's done.

"She might freeze me out and ignore me when I need her to respond."

"Haven't many of those things already happened?" I asked.

"Yes," Grace replied.

I responded, "It sounds to me as if Lauren is using you to vent her anger and frustration and you are using possibility thinking to make yourself crazy. While all of these concerns are certainly possibilities, I think you are most afraid of the possibility of losing your job and not having Lauren like you. So, you are losing sleep over possibilities that may never become realities or things that have happened but haven't changed anything."

I then challenged her, "What if, over the course of the next two weeks, you turned your phone on do not disturb and powered down your laptop after 6pm?"

"Uh, I don't know," Grace stammered.

"Here's the deal," I continued. "You are tired and, the more tired you are, the more anxious and insecure you become. And the more paralyzed you are to make important decisions. You need time to rest and re-energize. You can't keep going at this pace. As far as Lauren not liking you, it doesn't matter what you do for Lauren. She has already formed her opinion about you, good or bad. You aren't going to change that. Ironically, once someone makes up their mind about you, it is very infrequently changed—unless you get to know them on a very different level."

"I know that," Grace shared. "But it stresses me out to disconnect. You never know what Lauren might do or how she might react."

"Make sure she remembers that this was her idea," I said. "You might even tell Lauren in your weekly one-on-one meeting that you know that a lot is going on in the business and you need to start each day fresh eyed and ready for action. Inform her that you have had a meeting with your team and you all are going to start taking Lauren's sage advice to power down each evening, so you will be back and ready to roll at 9am! Then you have to do it, Grace. The first couple of nights will be difficult, but you will feel much more rested. Once you are more rested, I know you will feel better about taking steps to find a new environment and make the move."

I reinforced the benefits of retraining your brain. "This is the first step toward flipping your limiting belief of "I am too tired". Each time you have the desire to turn on your phone or laptop, remind yourself that you want to wake up tomorrow saying, 'I am *not* too tired—I am wide awake to tackle the day!' Once you are in a better place emotionally, John will feel less protective and reactive, too. Will you try it for the next three weeks?"

"I will do my best," Grace said.

"Great!" I said. "Now, I can't promise you that Lauren will not have her snarky moments or do something crazy that might derail what you have going on *but* you will be in a better place emotionally and will be looking for your next opportunity, so it may not get to you as much."

Over the course of the next three weeks, Grace did an amazing job at powering down. Lauren still had her moments of passive aggression and snark but Grace found that it wasn't getting to her as much anymore.

The next limiting belief that Grace tackled was "I am not worthy." Retraining this belief was an important step in being able to move on to a new environment and not repeating the mistakes of the past. Four months later, Grace moved on from Lauren and that toxic environment to a dream job and dream boss—and I'm happy to report that Grace is still there today. She continues to work through her limiting beliefs and tells me that she has become content with not being everyone's BFF but continues to make connections that count.

The belief wheel is critical to achieving your dreams and goals.

Belief shapes your reality and influences your behavior. Without belief, you are aimless and unfocused. You are less likely to change or take the steps toward your goals. You lose the drive to better yourself.

Taking stock of the limiting beliefs you have created over a lifetime of experiences helps chart a new path to help you ignite your passion, fuel your confidence to persevere and give you strength of will.

Another Approach to Belief: Meet Emma

Emma was referred to me by a friend who I had coached through a difficult family situation. Emma was hoping that I could help her navigate a relationship of her own, with the same success I'd had with her friend.

Emma was struggling with a co-worker, Ashleigh, whom she had worked with closely for several years. At one time, Emma had counted Ashleigh as a confidante. She'd invited Ashleigh into her home and the two had even gone on a couple of girl's weekends. From Emma's perspective, they were close friends.

Recently, Emma discovered that Ashleigh had been undermining her at work by gossiping about Emma behind her back. Considering their close relationship, Emma felt betrayed, particularly as the gossiping escalated to the point where Ashleigh was spreading lies about Emma to Emma's boss.

After speaking with Emma, her devastation was clear to me. She was having a very difficult time trying to understand how someone who was supposed to be a friend could outright lie about her to shared coworkers.

Emma even tried to take the matters into her own hands by confronting Ashleigh earlier in the week and Ashleigh denied saying anything to anyone. Ashleigh chalked the rumors up to immature co-workers and a poisonous work environment, and she even cried during their conversation while expressing her love, care, and friendship for Emma.

Emma was conflicted. She wanted to believe Ashleigh and believe in a friendship she held sacred. Emma had created a limiting belief by putting her faith in someone who did not deserve it. She created a fairytale in which she and Ashleigh were friends through thick and thin—no matter what. And although her gut told her otherwise, Emma's belief in the tale she told herself was tough to break.

After listening to Emma, it was clear to me that Ashleigh was not a friend but a frenemy. She saw herself not as Emma's trusted colleague and friend but as her rival vying for pole position. Ashleigh did not have Emma's best interest at heart.

In order for Emma to break free from the limiting belief she created, I needed to help Emma create a new story based in the reality of where their relationship lived now, not the sentimentality of the past.

"Emma, I know that you may not want to believe this, but the behavior that you are sharing about Ashleigh is that of a frenemy not a friend. Before you try to debate me on this, I want you to honestly answer a few questions, okay?" I asked.

"Okay," Emma shrugged.

"Does Ashleigh talk to others about you behind your back?" Although I knew the answer to this question, I wanted to draw attention to it once more.

"Yes," Emma said almost in a whisper.

"Who gets the better deal out of your relationship?" I asked. "Does Ashleigh ask you for more favors than you do for her? Are her emotional needs more frequent than yours?"

"Well yes," Emma said. "But that's only because she is a single mother who has a lot on her plate and things always seem to be blowing up in her life."

"Doesn't matter," I said. "Everyone has stuff in their life. But it's those who are constantly drowning in the me, me, me that get the better deal. Does Ashleigh talk more about herself and her life than you do yours?"

"Okay, I see where you are going with this," Emma said. "BUT again, she is a single mom with a lot on her plate."

"I get that," I said. "BUT again, everyone has the good, the bad and the in-between. Real friends have reciprocal sharing because they truly care about each other. Is Ashleigh happy about your accomplishments and your life?"

"I think so," Emma shrugged.

"Think about when you're together. Does Ashleigh seem genuinely happy when things are going well for you? Or does she quickly step over you to talk about herself?" I pressed.

"Well, Ashleigh has hurt my feelings at times because she doesn't take much time to give me a pat on the back or say she is happy for me, like I do for her," Emma replied.

"So she doesn't celebrate your accomplishments?" I asked.

"Not really," Emma admitted.

"What about competition?" I probed. "Does Ashleigh try to one-up you or minimize your successes, no matter how small or large?"

Emma thought a bit more, "Last week, I made significant progress toward a sale with a difficult client and, when I told the group in our meeting, Ashleigh couldn't wait to tell everyone that she had been instrumental in the deal. As if the calls she made were more important than my contributions."

"Would you consider Ashleigh to be passive-aggressive?" I asked.

"Very." Emma said.

"And last but not least, does Ashleigh enjoy drama?" I asked.

"Everything is dramatic to Ashleigh," Emma shared. "She's always worried that this person doesn't like her or that she's going to be taken off this account. Seems like she's always fighting with her family or coworkers. It's like she thrives on drama."

"Interesting," I replied. "You shared with me earlier that several coworkers have come to you about Ashleigh. All these individual accounts make it difficult for the rumors to be untrue. And most concerning is the call you received from your boss's close friend, who told you that Ashleigh has made frequent afterhours calls to your boss about you, and that the rumors she's spread are beginning to impact your boss's opinion of you.

"Are you ready to take back control of your life and put yourself first?" I asked.

"I know that I need to," Emma sighed. "Or my future at the company may be at risk. Not to mention a job that I love—it's worth fighting for."

Through her disloyalty, Ashleigh revealed herself to Emma and now it was up to Emma to rewrite her fairytale friendship to frenemy reality. It was time for Emma to get real. Only then could we craft a plan to deal with Ashleigh, minimize the damage she created at work and put Emma back in control of her emotions and her life.

Emma's Action Plan

Set boundaries with Ashleigh and stick to them!

- Keep conversation light and friendly
- Limit time together
- Minimize sharing personal information—discreetly shift their energy from confidante to acquaintance
- Gently drift apart over time

Check emotions at the door.

- Take a breath, don't let Ashleigh see you sweat

Keep work conversations "on the record."

- Be transparent and stick to group conversations or email, where Emma has the written word or others to back her up

- Communicate more openly, to alleviate the confusion or ambiguity of sidebar conversations

Keep ideas to yourself until it's time to present them.

- Respect your intellectual property — protect your ideas and eliminate any threat of Ashleigh taking credit for your accomplishments

Stay out of the sandbox and keep it professional

- Keep your frenemy status private — do not talk about Ashleigh with others
- Remember that, when you get into the sandbox with others, you risk getting sand in your eyes, which ultimately keeps you from seeing clearly!

Emma put her action plan into place and called me a few weeks later with an update. She was happy to report that Ashleigh had moved on from making trouble for Emma but dismayed that Ashleigh's behavior had not stopped entirely. Rather, she had found a new target at work.

Unsurprised, I shared an insight with Emma. Interestingly enough, Ashleigh's behavior is classic. A person as insecure as Ashleigh isn't easily deterred and rarely stopped. But over time, if the target of their attacks sticks to an action plan as Emma had, the Ashleighs of the world lose their captive audience and typically go silent or set their sights on someone more easily manipulated.

By flipping the script of her limiting belief, Emma regained her power and took control. Doing so laid the foundation for a happier, healthier life, inside the office and out.

Chapter 5

Passion is your mode of transportation.
Passion is your tennis ball. Anyone who knows me, knows that I love dogs. Their unwavering optimism and zest for life inspires me. And there isn't a creature alive who has more of it that my 10 pound miniature Schnauzer, Holly. She is passion personified. When she sees me take a yellow tennis ball from my pocket, the joy on her face is legendary. Her back legs turn to springs and her little body—not just her tail—

go into full, unabashed wag. When I throw the tennis ball to Holly, she returns it with the same intensity on throw 30 that she had on that first throw.

Now that's passion.

Or consider my nephew, John, whose passion was sharks. I have never seen someone so infatuated with sharks in my life—they were his obsession. From the time John was a little boy, he could tell you everything you could ever—and would ever—want to know about sharks. On a visit to any aquarium or library, he could pick every species of shark out of any saltwater tank or picture book. And don't get me started on *Jaws* or Shark Week. To this day, even as a grown man, John can recite the entire movie word-for-word, and Shark Week is like a national holiday in his household.

Pure passion.

Which brings me to you: What's your tennis ball? Do you have a Shark Week?

Let's dig deep again. Think about that one thing that, no matter how many times you talk about it or do it, brings you that feeling of unfiltered, uncontainable joy and purpose…every…single…time.

Meet your passion.

Passion and Belief

It's no surprise that passion and belief are besties. Sure they're incredible on their own but, when they get together, it's magic. Depending on where you start, the energy you create from one will transfer and ignite the other: The excitement you feel from being passionate about something fuels your belief. While belief may be the catalyst, or the starting point, the passion you have for your belief reinforces your direction and drive to pursue it.

Quite often, having a strong belief leads us to something that we become passionate about.

For example, you may not have thought about leading a charity drive when you began to volunteer. You simply believed in the charity's mission and wanted to help. But over time, because of your belief in the mission, a passion was born for stepping up and taking on the next drive.

Or you might believe that becoming an entrepreneur gives more work-life balance. The passion born from this belief is that you get truly excited when you help others build their own businesses—so excited that you can't hold back from talking with everyone about it. That's how powerful passion can be.

Passion is the force behind the validity of a belief. Passion is the force that puts you in forward motion to set goals and make it happen.

Think about someone you know who is living their dream. By investing in their passion, they made it central to their life's mission. Passion led them to success and happiness.

When you truly believe in something, your passion will help fuel the journey to your finish line, too.

The mind of a child is a great example of belief and passion at work in tandem.

When my son Aaron was in college, he won a 60-inch television in a raffle. It was Black Friday and we were shopping for presents while we were out of town for Thanksgiving. It was a big year—the new Xbox had just come out and the local game store had them in stock. He really wanted the new system for Christmas and asked me to purchase it that day and then "hold it" for him to open on Christmas morning. I was unsure about his proposal.

"You know I like to surprise you for Christmas and you like to be surprised, too," I said.

"But this time, I promise I will be okay with it," he assured me.

"I know you, and you won't be okay with it, and I don't want to schlep it back to Ohio," I replied.

"But I will be okay with it!" he retorted. "And if you wait, it will be out of stock and I won't get it. Then all of my friends will have it and be playing games and I will be left out."

Needless to say, his argument didn't convince me and I didn't buy the new Xbox that day. However, I did plan on purchasing it for Christmas. I just wanted it to be a surprise.

The following week, my son called me and told me that he had great news. He had sold the 60-inch television to someone and used the money to purchase a 32-inch television *and* the new Xbox system.

My son's belief was that the system would be out of stock and that he wouldn't be able to play with his friends. His passion for wanting the system was so great that it pushed him to think out of the box to overcome the obstacle he saw before him and cross his finish line.

When you truly believe in something, then you'll set a goal to shape that belief and, ultimately, lead you to your passion.

Belief and passion team up to allow you to explore opportunities and overcome obstacles. Simply put: Belief is the destination and passion is the mode of transportation.

When you are on the passion bus, you have a renewed energy. You want to be better and do better. And when your passion aligns with your values and personal brand, it becomes even more compelling because you create a platform that not only motivates you but inspires others, too.

Hyrum Smith, the co-founder and former CEO of Franklin Covey, built an illustrious career around the belief that, when your daily activities are in concert with your highest priorities, you have a credible claim to inner peace.

To fully develop your passion, you must hone your highest priorities. And the cool thing about connecting passion with priorities is that when you do, your daily path is in sync with your values and energy. Your daily path is grounded.

Passion and Your Personal Brand

It doesn't take an advertising icon to know that brands are boss. More than a logo or the latest shiny new toy, a brand transcends the physical to create an emotional connection that resonates long beyond the product experience.

The same is true for your personal brand. More than how you look or what you do, your brand is the experience of how others feel when you're with them. Like a lasting impression, your brand resonates well beyond your time together. It's the perception the world has of you—and it matters.

The way others see you is important in both sharing your passion and defining your brand because it's what they first think of when they hear your name. Your brand is your connection to showing your authentic self to the world.

Every once in a while, we encounter people

who are different. They seem special, but we don't exactly know why. They have a certain way of putting us at ease, as if they aren't out for anything else but to make a difference in our lives, personally.

What is it about these seemingly special people that sets them apart from countless others we meet?

In a word, *brand*. Their distinguishing difference is that they connect with us by heart and soul, because they are aligned with a higher purpose...they seem happier and healthier and even more productive than most people. And it's like magic.

We love to be around these people because they genuinely care about us, enjoy helping us and always leave us with good feelings. They unselfishly put us first, which creates loyalty that causes us to think of them before any others we know.

And when we think of them, we may even think of their business or cause because, over time, they have shown us that they can be counted on. We can trust them because we have connected with them in a special way.

We might be thinking, "I love Ella, she is amazing! I know that when I need skincare products, she is my go-to person." Or we might think of Matt, because Matt is always ready to help us with any DIY project. We might even call Ella our skin-care guru. Or Matt our DIY Project Master. People like Ella and Matt are unique because, from the time they wake up each day to when they turn in at night, is driven by their passion and personal brand.

In the case of Ella, her passion is making a difference in the lives of others. One good deed at a time, she puts her best face forward and inspires us to do the same for our skin. For Matt, his passion is helping others create a personal oasis in their own space, so they can energize and renew.

They live their lives and work their businesses from the heart and soul. And in the process of making it about others, they ultimately get what they want…simply by having a servant mindset.

Ella and Matt have created personal brands fueled by passion and, in doing so, they uniquely stand out from the rest. Ella and Matt are authentic. They know who they are, they live their truth and they lead with their passions.

Knowing who you are and what you stand for are the first steps in creating a personal brand that is fueled by your passion and driven by your belief.

Ella believes that everyone is doing the best they can. When she adds her passion for making a difference in the lives of others, Ella creates an unforgettable personal brand. Matt believes that small changes make for big impact. When he adds his passion for helping others to create a personal refuge, it's easy to see how they think of Matt when they want to renew.

Your passions are uniquely yours. They energize you and make you attractive to others. When you are clear about what moves or drives you, you can see new ways to link your passions to your beliefs, as well as to what you do and how you do it.

If you try to express your brand before you are clear about what moves or drives you, or how that connects to what is uniquely you, your time and effort won't be as productive.

Let's get back to inner peace. Think about this: People who have a strong personal brand are seemingly "special." They are the ones who are happy and who make us feel good when we are around them. They seem to have an inner peace because their daily path is in sync with their brand, and their brand is in sync with their highest priorities.

Personal brand is also about creating differentiation—it's about standing out. If what you offer is the same as everyone else who does what you do, you are a commodity. Common not irreplaceable—and you're better than that. Whether you are looking for friends or employers, knowing and living what makes you different is the secret to attracting the attention of those who are making a decision about you.

Personal brand is the way you show yourself to the world. Now more than ever, people crave authenticity. There are so many posers and players, and they all seem to ulterior motives that aren't driven by belief, passion or service. They don't lead with passion, live their truth or show their (or their company's) core values in the work they do, but instead try to manipulate by being someone they are not to close the deal.

These are not your people. And this is your opportunity to build your brand. And when you link it to your belief and passion, you will see a shift both in your business and in your life.

Passion: It's Your Superpower

Little kids dream of having superpowers. Big kids know they always had them. Your superpowers are the things that you do better than anyone else. Often, they are things you do with little effort. They are core to who you are. Some of us discount these strengths because we deliver these skills with little effort. But, like superpowers, they are a source of strength and purpose. When you are in your element, you have an energy about you. A passion. Your superpower will never exhaust you but always energize and excite you.

Several years ago, my boss pulled me aside

for a performance review. She asked me what I felt were my superpowers. I replied without hesitation that they were leading teams and strategic vision. While she agreed those were certainly strengths, she challenged me to get more granular. "Let me think for a moment," I said. "Okay, I believe my superpowers are insight and tenacity."

"Sure, I'll give you that", she said. "But I think your real superpowers are strength and humility. I have worked with countless executives over the years and I have never seen someone who is so strong yet so humble. This is truly your gift and what makes you such a great leader and connector."

I have never forgotten her words and, when difficult situations arise, I always take time to reflect on them. By helping me identify my superpowers, she sharpened by self-concept and changed the trajectory of my career.

One of my son Austin's superpowers is empathy. He has more insight into the feelings of others than anyone I have ever known. Because of this gift, he has garnered many deep connections and relationships built on great trust. Austin's friends know that he truly cares about them. Over the years, he has earned two "good citizen" awards at school, one for faith and one for kindness. His superpower of empathy has both driven these awards and, more importantly, shaped his relationships and views on the world. I couldn't be prouder of him.

My friend Susan has many superpowers, but the one that stands out most is her insatiable curiosity. Susan has an intense desire to really listen and learn to fully understand everything and everyone. This makes her both a wonderful friend and an excellent writer. She loves what she does and it shows. And her superpower of curiosity has helped her continuously evolve and grow while making all she touches feel loved and valued.

Now let's talk about you. What do you believe are your superpowers? If you need a little insight, ask your family and friends.

Passion and Values

Your values are your guiding principles. They affect how you feel, behave, and react. When you're aligned with your core values, you feel energized, confident, and open to others. And when you are out of alignment, you create a drag on your energy, lose focus, and shut down.

Think about a time when you were working against something you valued. You most likely felt exhausted, irritated, and anxious. We've all been there, and we don't care to go back. That's because, when you are working in concert with your values, you are living authentically and with passion.

Meet Tami

Tami came to me for coaching at a low point in her career. She recently made a significant move from a startup that she loved to take her first executive role with a larger company. The interview process with the larger company went well. She had numerous conversations with the executive team and really felt that her brand and values were in alignment with those of the company. Only a few short weeks into her role, she found out that the company was not living the values that they had lauded during her interviews. In fact, they were outright lying to their customers. Recent research showed that their products did not perform in the way that their literature and training stated. Although Tami gave recommendations on solutions for new messaging, the CEO did not feel new messaging was needed and asked executives to keep this confidential and continue sharing outdated, incorrect messaging and training. Since Tami was a company spokesperson, she came to work every day feeling like a fraud. Having to consistently guard the messaging when presented with questions exhausted her, and ultimately, affect her mental health. She became worried and anxious that, as an executive, she could be held complicit in the company's lies.

Ultimately through coaching, Tami was able to see that this position, albeit one that she had worked for many years to attain, was with the wrong company. Tami chose to reach out to her former employer who, after her departure clearly saw her value, welcomed Tami back. Over the next few months, Tami worked with the start-up's CEO to define new responsibilities that made both the CEO and Tami happy.

By realigning with her values, Tami returned to living with passion.

Passion and Purpose

Purpose is the foundation of passion.

Like your values, your purpose is connected to how you take what you value and turn it into your contributions to the world.

If belief is the destination and passion is the mode of transportation, then purpose is your *why*. It's your roadmap.

Having purpose helps you to identify what to pursue and what to avoid.

When your passion is not connected to belief and lacks purpose, you risk losing your way and burning out. This is why people who are going through a major life crisis tend to feel aimless and uncertain.

For example, let's take an interest like volunteerism. If you register donors at the local blood drive, you are probably passionate about volunteerism. But if you are recruiting blood donors for the local blood drive, you're likely passionate about volunteerism *and* fulfilling your purpose of saving lives.

The magic is in the balance. In getting your passion and purpose to align.

Go back to your interest in volunteerism. If your belief is that too many people die every day from lack of blood donations and your passion is volunteerism and your purpose is to save lives, then your belief, passion, and purpose are in alignment. They complement each other and elevate the impact of your work.

Purpose takes action. If your belief is that too many people die every day from lack of blood donations and your purpose is to save lives and yet you do nothing about it, then nothing is aligned, the connection is lost and your purpose is aimless.

Be a Goal Getter

It's easier than you might think. There's an interest that we hold in each passion and belief—it is why we're motivated by them. Need a motivational boost? Look to your passions and beliefs. They are great motivational triggers that inspire you to set and strive for goals.

Nothing happens from doing nothing, right?

No matter how you begin, passions and beliefs will always require action to be successful. One will always influence the other, so execute passion in all that you do and start to believe in what you can achieve. Allow your passion to encourage your belief and encourage your belief to pursue you passion.

Back to Your Tennis Ball

The trick is finding your tennis ball. It's out there waiting for you to discover.

Start with the Passion Grid (Appendix—The Four Wheels Tool Box), which will help you take a deeper dive into the fuel that drives you and connects you to your personal brand. Be open, honest and ready to unlock your passion. It's in there!

Chapter 6

If belief is the destination and passion is the mode of transportation, skill is your compass. Think of it as the road rules for staying on course as you encounter pot holes along your journey.

Resilience feeds skill, so let's get equipped with the tools you need to make the journey meaningful and successful—and fun. Never lose sight of that.

Interestingly enough, skill is one of the most

frequent reasons people come to me for coaching, yet it's one of the most infrequent reasons for their struggles.

Skill can be tricky because it can be deceiving. In my coaching conversations, I frequently hear people tell me that skill was holding them back but, when pressed in the coaching process, they come to the realize that their struggle was really rooted in one of the other wheels (belief, passion or will) and not a lack of skill.

Over the years, I began to see similarities in the behaviors and mindset of those I coached who thought that their lack of skill was holding them back. I started to create whimsical character names for these traits, so that those I coached could connect to the real issue more easily and develop a better understanding of what was actually holding them back. Taking on a character allowed them to tackle the issue at hand and move forward, not get stuck in the defensive.

The Expert

Have you ever stopped yourself from doing something because you weren't good at it or because someone else you were working with was better at it than you? Rest assured, you're not alone.

I can relate. My husband is an excellent golfer and I am, well, *not*. I am also an overachiever with dashes of perfectionism and competitiveness. I like to do everything well and win. When I realized that I had very little chance of ever beating my husband, I decided that I simply didn't want to play golf with him.

Interestingly enough, the Expert is a self-limiting prophecy. You will never become an expert at anything unless you actually try.

The Expert is driven by fear of failure, which stems from a limiting belief. If you are the Expert, you want to take the time to evaluate and determine which limiting belief is holding you back. Only then can you begin to see things from a different perspective.

For me, I had to let go of "I will never beat him" and change my perspective to "Golfing is a great way to spend time together." Because that's what really matters.

The Procrastinator

The Procrastinator says that they really want to learn but something is always in their way. They will do almost anything or come up with any excuse to avoid actually buckling down and learning something new.

You might hear the Procrastinator say things like, "I will start the training as soon as the holidays are over" or "If I felt better this week I would do it" or "I need to organize my office because, when I have everything in order, I can do it."

When my friend Maggie heard me talk about the Procrastinator, she shouted over the phone, "That's me!" She told me that, when the opportunity to learn something new came up, her first thought was always that it had to be a perfect learning scenario. Her office had to be in order, the kids had to be quiet, she needed to have had a good night's sleep, and it had to be early enough in the day. As you can imagine, she found that these things rarely aligned so she never really got to learning something new.

The Procrastinator creates their own paralysis by the very thought of taking the action steps to learn and grow. Procrastinators are typically people pleasers who take on more than they can handle, or they are plagued with a self-limiting belief like "I am not tech savvy" or "I have never been great at learning."

Sound familiar? If you are a Procrastinator, you want to focus on the root of your procrastinating tendencies, so you can move past them and make progress toward your goal.

After Maggie and I talked, she found out that the Procrastinator in her stemmed from the fact that she had too much on her plate and she had always struggled with Attention Deficit Disorder. Over the years, she had convinced herself that she simply wasn't good at studying. When we were able to take some things off her workload and create a plan where she could learn in manageable chunks of time, her learning—and her confidence—soared.

The Armchair Quarterback

The Armchair Quarterback can tell you all the reasons why the new training or ideas are wrong, won't work and why their way of doing things is better.

Armchair Quarterbacks are ego focused and are tough to coach. You might hear an Armchair Quarterback say things like, "I don't need to learn this, I'm already an expert," "I tried it and it doesn't work" (not true), "Management never understands what we need," or "I don't know why they didn't ask my opinion first."

Armchair Quarterbacks look for sympathetic ears so that they can rally the troops to their cause. They blindly create a mob mentality because they are passionate about their position.

A few years ago, David came to me for coaching. He was struggling with a new training program that his company had recently launched. He wanted my help in finding the strategic positioning and words to convince his company that they needed to change this program and incorporate his ideas. After all, he had been with the company for 23 years. He had taken the new training and it was horrible (limiting belief). Although he was getting paid to take the training, the company just didn't get it. David felt the executives' ideas were ridiculous and, even worse, the new company-required reporting was a time waster. He already didn't have enough hours in his week to add more to his plate.

After listening to David, I pressed him for specific details about the training. His responses were generic, which supported my suspicion that he hadn't taken the training in its entirety. After some contemplation, I thought it might be helpful to have him reframe his perspective about the new training. I asked him if he would be open to an activity. He said that he would do anything if I could help him to help the company see their shortcomings.

I asked him how long it took someone to complete the new training program. He shared that it would take someone two weeks if they took a course or two each day. I shared that, since I hadn't seen the training, it was difficult for me to help him with his positioning. If he really wanted my perspective, it would be helpful for him to take the training and make notes in each segment identifying areas of opportunity. Once I had a clear understanding of the gaps, I would be in a better position to help him.

David agreed and we set a time to meet

again in two weeks.

When we met again, I found that David had many well thought out notes on the training. Over the next few coaching sessions, I helped David take his notes and break down the limiting thoughts and beliefs that he had around the training. Over time, David began to see the value in much of the training and found a few areas of opportunity that he was able to share respectfully with his supervisor.

The Status Quo

The Status Quo can tell you all the reasons why we should have never changed things in the first place.

The Status Quo is stuck, afraid of change and struggling with fear of failure. You might hear the Status Quo say things like, "I don't know why they keep changing everything when it's not broken," "It has been like this since 2009 and we like it that way," or "Why add all these bells and whistles? They aren't necessary."

Status Quos are often more passive and don't openly admit they are not receptive to change. They sit back and read the room to validate their thoughts and feelings.

Andy was an independent business owner in the direct selling industry. He was a highly regarded sales leader who had been with the company for 12 years and through many product changes. Recently, the company had replaced his favorite product with a newer version and he was frustrated. It made no sense to him and he was struggling. The new product said that it was improved, yet some of the things that he liked about the old product (and that made him and his customer's loyal buyers) were not incorporated into the new product. Andy couldn't understand or embrace the change and called me to vent.

"We are going to lose loyal customers over this, Lisa. The company is going to lose millions," (limiting belief) he said. "They always thumb their nose at their loyal customers and reps. My customers and I have used this product for 12 years and it's the only product out there that does what this does. Everyone else seems excited about this new product, even you Lisa, and I can't believe it when you know how much we sell of the tried-and-true product."

"Andy," I replied. "I can understand that change is difficult. But that is life and business. I haven't heard anything from you that tells me that the new product won't give you everything that the earlier version did. I have even heard some new and improved benefits."

I then asked Andy to make a list of the pros and cons of the original formula versus the new formula. We sat together over the phone and I helped Andy work through his thoughts. After he made an extensive list, we reviewed it together.

"Andy, you started our conversation telling me that you are going to lose loyal customers over this formula change. You also said that the company will lose millions. After reviewing the vast list of benefits, do you still feel that way?"

"Okay, you got me," he said. "I see what you are trying to do. You wanted me to see that I was overreacting."

"Yes, Andy, but I also wanted you to see that you have 12 years of experience in this business. You are a highly respected leader. I needed you to see that you had the skill and knowledge to not only work through the change yourself, but to help your loyal customers to do the same." I simply reassured him that he is resilient.

Working through the Status Quo's fear of change by showing them that they are not as ill equipped as they might believe helps them reframe their limiting beliefs and recalibrate to a positive, productive path.

The Ready, Willing, and Ables

The Ready, Willing, and Ables are self-aware and can easily articulate the skills where they fall short. They are open to learning new things. They have emotional maturity and understand that they can't know everything about everything. They understand their areas of opportunity and are open to evaluation and assessment of their skills—and they look at feedback as a gift.

The Ready, Willing, and Ables are a dream to coach, train, and develop. I do mental cartwheels when I encounter someone who is ready, willing, and able because I know we are going places together! It's really exciting—and it's where I want you to be.

You've Got This!

If you see yourself in any of the characters, then give yourself an "A" for self-awareness. You're on your way.

The first step in making lasting change is acknowledgment. The beautiful thing about skill is that if you have the determination and motivation, you can learn to be better and do better. You don't have to stay in the same place, with the same skills, getting the same results. You can learn and grow—and have fun doing it. You just have to seek out change and stay open while making it. I believe in you.

Chapter 7

If belief is the destination, passion is the mode of transportation, and skill is your road rules, then *will* is getting behind the wheel. (And off the couch!)

So are you willing? Your will is your level of engagement and the way you make things happen in life and in your business. And it's a powerful thing.

Will is our driving force. Will creates motion and momentum. Will stops us from giving up. Will gets the job done. And only you can determine yours.

Think of will as electrical because it has power. You alone direct that power the way you desire. Your will is the inner energy that controls this behavior. Consider this: All habits, good or bad, are the result of your will to do them. Every time you accomplish any act, whether conscious or unconscious, you use the power of your will.

And the way you use your will makes all the difference in your life's outcome.

Have you ever asked yourself, "Why won't I just do it?" or "Why don't I want this as much as I should?" Or perhaps your spouse, partner, or friend asks you, "Why do I want this for us more than you do?"

In my coaching, I see these same scenarios play out. "I just wish they would do it" or "Why don't they want it for themselves?" or, even better, "Why do I feel like I want this more than they do?"

Remember, people tend to stay motivated when they see the value in the things that they want to do or are asked to do. Think of yourself. Do you tend to lose focus when you can't see the bigger picture? If you're like most, you hear that little voice in your head asking, "What's in it for me?" It's a fair question—and a key insight into your will.

The reason your friend skips the girls' night you planned or your colleague backs out of the meeting you worked so hard to prepare for is very simple: They don't see the benefits and rewards they will receive by being there.

When it comes to someone's level of engagement, remember that most accomplishments take some work—and some take a heap of hard work. And the more hard work or the greater the contribution, they more benefits or rewards they need to reap in order to remain engaged.

It's a simple value proposition, really.

The key to getting someone to "get off the couch" is to help them understand the value in what they will be doing. Their value proposition is the benefits and rewards they receive relative to the time and effort they put forth.

When determining will, here are three questions to ask:

○ Question 1: What's in it for ME?
○ Question 2: Is it WORTH it?
○ Question 3: Can I DO it?

What's In It for Me? (Or WIFM)

It's basic psychology, really. Most human beings need to see what they get relative to the work and time they put in.

So how do we motivate the unmotivated? We show them what's in it for them.

When I think about this, that famous scene from the movie "Jerry McGuire" always comes to mind. You remember the one. Football player Rod Tidwell repeatedly yells at Jerry to "show me the money!"

WIFM is very much like this. To motivate someone to get them to go "all in" we need to "show them the value!" That's the WIFM.

And if there isn't something in it for them—if they can't see the value—they aren't going to commit.

To see this in action, think about your business. Are your meetings or coaching calls and conversations giving everyone what they need? Do your meetings reach across all levels? Is there new information to share or are you simply rinsing and repeating because you feel obligated to meet? If your team hears the same message over and an over, then it should be no surprise if engagement is low. Do you keep up on current trends and what your competition is doing, so that your coaching and training is relevant? Or are you on autopilot, recycling the same training you've done for the past several years?

Let's dig a little deeper. Are you balancing training and follow-up with inspiration, motivation and team building? It's easy to do a quick WIFM check in to see if you are hitting the marks.

Think for a moment about the relationship you have with someone on your team. This someone may report to you or may be someone you coach or mentor. In your journal, write their name at the top of a page.

On the left-hand side of the page, list all the contributions you are making to this relationship. What you are GIVING. This list might include things like observations where you give feedback, one-on-one calls, or helping them frame out a plan for their overall professional development. Title this list "What I Give."

On the right-hand side of the page, make a second list, and title it "What I Get." Write all of the benefits that YOU are RECEIVING. Things like they need little supervision, they are hitting their goals and other benefits of your relationship.

Now sit back and compare the two lists. Resist the urge to count the number of items to compare, since chances are you may have left something off the list. Instead, answer this question: Considering all that you give to this relationship versus all that you're getting from it, who is getting the better deal?

Your answer will be one of the following:
- *"I am getting a better deal."* If this is your answer, it can lead to complacency and ingratitude from both you and your team member.
- *"The other person is getting the better deal."* If this is your answer, it will produce resentment for both you and your colleague.
- *"We are getting an equally good deal."* If this is your answer, it will produce the mutual respect and motivation that will keep the relationship going.

Now that we have reviewed someone at work, let's move on to someone in our personal life.

Think for a moment about the relationship you have with someone in your life. This could be your spouse, significant other or a friend.

In your journal, write their name at the top of a page.

On the left-hand side of the page, list all the contributions you are making to this relationship. What you are GIVING. This list might include things like "I do the laundry," "I cook nightly dinner," "I get the kids off to school," and "I pay the bills." Title this list "What I Give."

On the right-hand side of the page, make a second list, and title it "What I Get." Write all of the benefits that YOU are RECEIVING. Things like they take care of the yard, they jump in so I can do girls' night, and other benefits of your relationship.

Now sit back and compare the two lists. Again, don't count the number of items to compare, since chances are you may have left something off the list. Instead, answer this question: Considering all that you give to this relationship versus all that you're getting from it, who is getting the better deal?

Your answer will be one of the following:
- *"I am getting a better deal."* If this is your answer, it can lead to complacency and ingratitude from both you and the other person.
- *"The other person is getting the better deal."* If this is your answer, it will produce resentment for both you and the other person.
- *"We are getting an equally good deal."* If this is your answer, it will produce the mutual respect and motivation that will

keep the relationship going.

In reviewing your answers on both lists, when you know for sure that each of you is getting an equally good deal, your engagement should be high, as each party is getting rewarded based on the effort they are putting in.

When your answers show that you are putting in more time and effort than the other person, then it's time to have a conversation with the other party. The caveat here is that you want to make sure that your perception of things isn't biased. Someone's perception can be their reality, so in these cases it would be helpful to give the other person this activity and compare their perspective to yours. There will also be times that deep down you know you aren't getting the benefit and this list confirms it. No conversation will change things so you have a decision to make.

If you are a supervisor, mentor, or coach, then you may have to make the difficult decision of ending someone's employment or the coaching relationship.

If the other party is a spouse, significant other or friend, then it can be a bit trickier. Talking to a licensed professional can help you to navigate next steps.

Let's go back to the business scenario. When you know for sure that each of you is getting an equally good deal, chances are you will see an increase in performance and attendance to meetings and coaching calls. You will also see an improvement in the way those on your team react and respond to you, and in the way they engage in their business.

And in your personal life, when both parties are getting an equally good deal, then relationships are stronger and couples and friends are happier.

Meet Carrie

Carrie was an independent business owner who came to me because her business was declining. Between her full-time job, her business, and her home life, she was exhausted and frustrated. Her team was inactive and she wasn't getting the support at home that she needed. She was ready to throw in the towel.

"I am so tired of these people asking me for coaching and training and not showing up," Carrie lamented. "Then they have the audacity to complain to me that they aren't making enough and they want to quit. And quite honestly, Matt is driving me crazy. He actually told me last night that he didn't want to babysit the kids while I was on a Zoom call with my team! Babysit? His own kids? Really? And then after all the arguing with Matt, only one person showed up for my Zoom call. I want to cry."

I could tell that Carrie's frustration was at DEFCON 1. After talking her off the ledge a bit, I asked her to do two things:
- Send me the agenda for your Zoom call to review
- Complete the Giving and Receiving ac-

tivity with Matt

This was what I received from Carrie:

Monthy Team Meeting Agenda, Friday, 7-8:40

- 7-7:30   Check In (how are folks doing?)
- 7:30-8:15 Product Training
- 8:15-8:25 Call to Action (schedule their own team meeting to give the product training to their own teams and share the dates)
- 8:25-8:40 Inspirational Close (TED Talk, "Inside the Mind of a Master Procrastinator")

Give and Receive List

What I Give (Carrie)

Wakes up 3 kids for school each day
Makes their breakfast
Packs their lunches
Drives 2 kids to school
Goes to work to help with family finances
Make dinner
Cleans up house
Loads and unloads dishwasher
Does laundry

Works my direct sales business to help with family finances:
 	
    Selling
    Sponsoring
    Customer Service
    Creating Training
    Team Meetings
    Coaching, etc.

Helps kids with homework
Reviews grades weekly online
Shops for groceries
Takes kids to doctor appointments
Takes kids to extra-curricular activities
Gets kids moving for church on Sunday
Calls repair services and anything else that happens in the home

What I Receive (Matt)

Drives 1 kid to school
Works to help support family
Sometimes grills in summer months
Does lawn work
Does his own laundry
Sometimes "babysits" kids begrudgingly
Attends kids' games

After I reviewed Carrie's team meeting agenda, I offered the following notes:

Monthly Team Meeting Agenda Friday 7:00-8:40 PM	
Is this a typical agenda for you?	
Check In (How is everyone doing?) *Asking everyone to "round robin" check in can be uncomfortable for some and very time consuming.*	7:00 – 7:30
Training (Product Training) *Does everyone see product training as valuable?* *Does the company provide product training elsewhere?* *Where are you getting the product training to share with your team?* *Is this redundant?*	7:30 – 8:15
Call to Action (Schedule their own team meeting to give the product training to their team – Everyone shares their dates) *Sharing a meeting date is a passive call to action and may not net you the results you want*	8:15 – 8:25

Inspirational Close (TED Talk – Inside the mind of a Master Procrastinator) *Does this fit with your meeting topic?* *It is a long close that may not see like a value add* *May be better to share this as a "I highly recommend" or a "to-do" after the call for those who want it*	8:25 – 8:40

Carrie and I discussed my notes on her team meeting agenda.

Carrie had been using this agenda with her team meetings for the past two years and her team had long ago stopped attending. Although she had more than 50 active team members, her highest attendance over the past year had been three.

After our discussion, Carrie understood that, although she was "giving" much information on her team Zoom, it was clear that her team didn't think that both parties were getting an equally good deal when they attended her meetings.

Carrie was spending too much time preparing for her meetings and creating much of her own training. This was making her feel stressed out, anxious and under-valued. When I asked if the company provided product training, she said yes but she felt that most people didn't take the training, and that she helped to give a different perspective.

Her virtual meetings had become long and rather uninteresting.

She agreed that her call to action was passive and not results oriented, but she too had become more passive in her call to action when her team stopped attending.

I explained to Carrie that, instead of changing her call to action plan, she needed to change her overall agenda. Her team had stopped attending because they weren't seeing the value in taking time out of their schedules to make the meeting.

In addition, Carrie was spending too much time re-creating the wheel. If the company had product training, she didn't need to duplicate their efforts.

One of the best ways to show value in bringing teams together is to focus on what they need at that moment in time. Because this can be a bit different for everyone, focusing on the issues at hand helps the collective group decide which issues are important while allowing the leader to focus their attention on solutions.

One way to think about this is that, as parents, we don't want our children living with us when they are 40, so from an early age, we are coaching them to be independent problem solvers who can tackle challenges and move forward with confidence.

In my family, my boys know that it's more important to come with solutions to the problems they face than with the problems alone.

That's why they know my response will always be, "Don't come to me with problems, come with solutions." To this day, they'll say, "Mom, I have a problem…but I also have an idea for a solution." Now, I can't say that their solutions are always ideal, but focusing forward kick-starts their thinking, empowers them and allows me to be a better coach to them.

With this in mind, I shared with Carrie how she could take 30 minutes bi-weekly or monthly to bring her team together and inspire them to help each other. It wouldn't take her much effort at all, because while she would be the facilitator and coach, her team would be training and problem solving together. This approach would ensure that her team meetings were mutually beneficial and with the attendance and engagement that she wanted.

30-Minute "In and Out and Nobody Gets Hurt" Team Meeting Agenda	
Good News!	5 Minutes
Beat on the Street	10 Minutes
Solve to the Beat on the Street	10 Minutes
Call to Action	2 Minutes
Inspirational Close	3 Minutes

When you let your team know that you will be moving to a 30-minute "In and Out and Nobody Gets Hurt" Team meeting, you set a productive, positive tone for your agenda right off the bat. Most people can give up 30 minutes of their time and because "nobody gets hurt" the content feels unimposing and comfortable.

Meetings should always start with "Good News" because it helps to reinforce the tone. Your team starts off optimistic, which creates a positive mindset for the training to come. Don't get hung up on the topics of "Good News"— you don't really care if their good news is that the sun is shining or that they have a new baby on the way. Remember that your goal is simply to set a positive tone. As time moves on and the team begins to have business progress, you will find that they will start to share more organically. And as a leader, you can always share a bit of good business news to point them in a different direction.

Once you've set the tone, you want to move to the "Beat on the Street." This is the barometer for how things have been going. The idea is to take the group's temperature. How is the group feeling? Are things going well or not so well with their respective businesses? If you are working with corporate teams, this still applies, but your team may share things like, "The system crash had us working after-hours and caused some other issues," or "We had a record number of shipments this week."

Once you know the "Beat on the Street" you want to ask your team which issues they feel are most important. More than likely, they will choose to focus on one or two of the challenges mentioned by the group. With these issues identified, you will spend the rest of the time allotted to solving the "Beat on the Street."

For example, if your team focuses on a system crash, you might talk through ways to avoid this in the future or how you might help those who are still behind catch up.

Once you have worked through your solutions to the "Beat on the Street", you want to share a call to action. If you remember, Carrie's call to action was very passive—she asked her team to schedule their own team meeting and to let her know when they will hold it. No one was held accountable to actually holding the meeting so they could have said anything.

Make sure that your call to action is both action oriented and backed by accountability. Let's say that your team was struggling with getting appointments booked on their calendars. You talked through ideas and words to overcome this, then your call to action might be:

- In the next 48 hours, reach out to five people to book an appointment or sales call.
- Note your results and share them in our group chat or with someone on the call to hold you accountable.
- In two weeks, report your great results as "Good News" on our next call.

Your call to action should only take a minute or two and can be posted on a group chat or on the white board in the common area of the office.

Once everyone has their marching orders,

it's time to close the meeting.

Finding something inspirational is as easy as asking someone to share one big goal that they accomplished since the previous meeting and how they got there. Or you can choose someone to highlight that week or simply drawing a random name and say something positive about them. Your goal is to end the meeting on a positive note.

Over the years, I have used and coached to the 30-Minute "In and Out and Nobody Gets Hurt" Meeting and it has never let me (or those I have coached) down. This proven framework makes coaching look easy and gives your team what they need, when they need it most. Every. Time.

Now back to Carrie. After reviewing her team meeting agenda, Carrie and I moved to her "Give and Receive" lists. Upon a quick read-through, it was clear to me that Carrie felt she was doing the bulk of the work at home.

I asked Carrie where she thought there may be areas of opportunity in her list. Did she see any areas on either side that could be combined, disseminated elsewhere or re-visited by both parties? Carrie said that re-visiting the list wasn't an option. Matt just wouldn't listen.

"Okay," I said. "What about combined or disseminated? After all, your kids are getting older. Can they help out?" (Her daughter Jordan was 5, son Sam was 7 and daughter Haley was 12). "Haley is 12 now and in middle school. Could she set her alarm clock in the morning and wake Jordan and Sam? She might even help you tag-team breakfast or lunch. This could really help Haley feel as if she was growing up. Jordan and Sam are not toddlers, either. They can certainly help you with the dishwasher and some household chores apart from their rooms. You might consider having a family board meeting (Appendix) to get everyone on the same page. If Matt sees the kids stepping up, he might begin to think differently."

"I have wanted to hold a family meeting for a while now," admitted Carrie. "But I just didn't know how to approach it. I would really like your help with this." I walked Carrie through the family board meeting and she agreed to hold the meeting later that week.

Carrie and I reconnected a couple of weeks later and she shared that she had made some positive changes. She held her first team meeting and had nine attend. While it wasn't the number she'd hoped for, it was better than it had been over the past year. She got great reviews and a lot of buzz on their team chat. She felt like the next meeting would be better.

Carrie had her family meeting and although Matt attended, he was more of a silent observer. The kids were excited about taking on their new responsibilities. Carrie hoped that over time, Matt would change his tune.

"Give him time," I said. "Perhaps asking him for help in one area will give him the boost he needs. For example, you could ask him to throw in a load of the kid's laundry when he does his own."

A week later, Carrie reported that Matt was now doing all the laundry. He hadn't done the laundry in the past because he thought Carrie was particular and didn't want his help. He was even teaching Sam how to do his own laundry, too. Progress!

Carrie's example proves that, when reviewing activities on the "receive" list, you should always consider whether or not you have expressly asked the other person for their help or participation. You don't get what you don't ask for.

For instance, you are coaching someone and put on your list that you give your time and they don't show up, have you clearly laid out the consequences when they miss your call? Have you set specific parameters around your coaching?

When someone coaches with me, I require the following:

○ They call me at their designated coaching time (or join me on Zoom).

○ They are considered "on-time" until five minutes after the hour.

○ Once they are more than five minutes late, I give their coaching slot to someone else on my waitlist.

○ If they miss more than three coaching calls in a row, they have to "wait out" from coaching with me for six months.

○ I send each person I coach a short recap of what we discussed, which includes "food for thought" items as well as their homework assignment.

- In order to schedule a subsequent coaching call, they must complete their homework and send it to me by the homework deadline.

Remember, when it comes to coaching and development, the leader can't be the only one with skin in the game. Many leaders have a loose and fast coaching framework that neither creates value for the person being coached nor holds them accountable to their commitments. When we create a solid framework and hold others accountable, most people will adapt. Those who don't are probably not coachable or worth your time.

Is It Worth It?

With this question, one wants to know that the time/effort/energy they spend on something is relative to what they get in return for their efforts. Assessing worth can be tricky—and answering this question with a "yes" starts by connecting your heart to your goal. Ask yourself:

- "How will I feel at the end of the month when I achieve ... ?"
- "What will my family think when I achieve this goal?"
- "Who is the first person I will call when I get ... ?"
- "What am I willing to do to get ... ?"
- "Why is the goal important to me?"

Can I Do It?

The interesting thing about this question is that it comes down to confidence. Here's where skill versus will comes into play.

The following questions will help tackle insecurity, to determine if you feel equipped to achieve your goal. Ask yourself:

- "Do I believe I have the skills and resources to achieve my goal?"
- "How best can I be supported in achieving my goal?"

If you are coaching someone through this question, you want to help them decide—success is ultimately in their hands. To alleviate their insecurities, walk them through it.

Get off the Couch!

Plenty of people have great plans that never come to fruition. Maybe you're reading this and you have a great idea or thought that popped into your mind but you pushed it aside because life got in your way or you felt it was silly or too "out there." Perhaps the very thought of what you are trying to do is paralyzing—it feels too daunting to even get started.

Be gentle with yourself. We all get stuck sometimes, make excuses and even spend too much time concocting a master plan versus taking that first step.

Is our master plan always easy? No!

Trust me, there will be storms, tigers, sharks,

fires, snakes, tornados, and bears that get in our way, but that's life. If we let obstacles stop us from achieving our dreams, we end up with a whole lot of what-ifs:

What if I had only done...
What if it had gone this way...
What if I had changed this or that...

What-ifs suffocate our will to get things done. To accomplish all that we are capable of.

I can relate. More about that in a bit.

Sometimes it's easier to sit on the couch than it is to get up and take a step. Keep in mind that the size of your step doesn't matter, you simply have to take it.

Chapter 8
Put The Wheels in Motion: Meet Lizzie

It's no secret that the only constant in life is change. When you have someone who is all in and willing to do the work, it's a beautiful thing to watch them put all four wheels into motion.

Such is the case with Lizzie.

Lizzie was at a crossroads in her life. The kind of struggle that caused her to question everything, at work and in life.

What once brought Lizzie joy, purpose, and fulfillment suddenly felt flat, mundane, and tedious. She was disenchanted, disconnected, and distant—like so many of us, Lizzie had allowed her work to consume so much of her energy that her relationships were suffering. Where she once enjoyed a work-life balance, she now wallowed in exhaustion. She found herself putting off activities and events she knew would be memorable and meaningful, only to face a workload that never lightened in a work environment that had become toxic. Lizzie's kids were tired of promises not kept, her husband found ways to fill his life without her, and the friends she once felt deeply connected to had moved on.

The thoughts, actions and plans that had been the very fuel to Lizzie's success now had her in a state of "autopilot"—she was going through the motions rather than living her best life. And although she attempted a few course corrections here and there, she just couldn't get it together.

Lizzie was lost.

She felt alone, defeated, and regretful. Like the driver who can't see their destination because of windshield glare, she was blinded by sun spots in her eyes. Lizzie knew she needed to pull over, but what then? Would she ever get back on the road? She longed for a way out but wondered if that road even existed or if she would have the courage to take it.

One night while lying in bed saying her prayers, Lizzie's thoughts kept coming back to the Four Wheels: Belief, Passion, Skill, Will. Belief, Passion, Skill, Will. SWOT, Board of Directors. Board of Directors, SWOT.

Why now? Why these words? Like a meditation, Lizzie repeated them over and over until she finally opened her daily journal and wrote the following words, "I am not on the right path. I need help. I need to find my path and myself again."

Lizzie woke the next morning with a newfound sense of purpose, as if a weight had been lifted. While making breakfast for her son, they made plans for the weekend. Plans that she knew would not be broken, although her son was skeptical. Once her son was out the door, Lizzie went to her office and opened a notebook. At the top of the page she wrote the words *My SWOT*. She then drew a box with four squares. In the first square she wrote "Strengths." In the second, she wrote "Weaknesses." In the third, "Opportunities" and in the fourth, "Threats."

She stared at the blank page for what seemed like hours, only to feel more defeated. She dug deep, searching for that belief she once had in herself. Determined, Lizzie got up from her office chair and decided to go for a walk. As she walked, the meditative rhythm of her thoughts on the Four Wheels aligned with each step: "I am not on the right path. I need help. I need to find myself again."

Lizzie took out her phone and in the notes typed the words again. "I am not on the right path. I need help. I need to find my path and myself again."

She continued to walk for what seemed like a very long time in the quiet. After a while, she opened a playlist and clicked on the first song.

Like a battle cry from the universe, it was *Brave* by Sara Bareilles. It was another epiphany.

As Lizzie listened to the song, she began to feel the same sense of purpose that she felt earlier that day. She opened notes in her phone and typed:

"I am stuck. I am NOT stuck."
"I am defeated. I am a WINNER."
"I am not present. I am PRESENT."

As she made her way back home, Lizzie repeated the phrases in her head, only to realize that what got her stuck in her SWOT was that the strengths others had lauded within her—the same strengths that had always given her a sense of confidence and competence—seemed completely lost to her. Somewhere along the way, she pushed aside her strengths for feelings of defeat and self-doubt.

Lizzie thought, "Just because I haven't seen some of these strengths lately, doesn't mean that they aren't within me. I need to rediscover them. I can do this." She went back to her desk, set to tackle her SWOT with a new perspective: "Write my SWOT based on the things that my colleagues, friends and family have shared about me over my lifetime and career. Whether I think they're true today or not, I know that I have these strengths in me somewhere."

Here's what transpired:

Strengths *(Things you do well, positive personality traits, achievements)*	**Weaknesses** *(Negative work habits or personality traits, things you avoid)*
Loving Giving Persuasive Focused Extroverted Collaborative Relationship Driven Communicator Motivator Creative & Optimistic Flexible/Adaptable Respectful	Self-criticism Can't say no Disconnected Trust everyone Socially isolated Lack of time
Opportunities *(Resources, tools, training or networking groups that you participate in; things you do for you/personal and professional growth)*	**Threats** *(Obstacles, challenges or threats to your business or personal life)*
Read 2 books per week Journal every day Mentor meeting Networking group Church	I don't make others who I value a priority because I know that they will forgive I assume that everyone thinks as I do I allow work to take priority in my life

Lizzie looked at what she had written. She read her SWOT over and over, then took a break, poured a glass of wine and asked herself one question: "Why?"

After some thought, she began to write: *Why have I lost my joy for my work and my life? Why have I allowed others to rob me of my strengths and achievements? Why do I allow myself to put the needs of others before my own? Why do the thoughts of others who aren't in my inner circle mean more to me than the thoughts of those who I love and hold dear?*

Lizzie read and reread her answers and felt an overwhelming surge of emotion. It was now so clear to her. Lizzie was allowing her weaknesses, not her strengths, to drive her journey.

Self-criticism
Can't say no
Disconnected
Trust everyone
Socially isolated
Lack of time

Putting her weaknesses at the wheel left Lizzie vulnerable to not only derailing her journey but losing everything and everyone that she had worked for and valued throughout her life.

I don't make others who I value a priority because I know that they will forgive.

I allow work to take priority in my life.

Lizzie knew she had been prioritizing the wrong things. Because her intentions were good, she assumed that family and friends would forgive her when she put them aside. Although she always intended to make it up to them, she rarely did. People stopped believing her, so much so that she stopped believing in herself.

As Lizzie looked at her threats, she remembered the words of one of her mentors, "You can get another job but can you get another family?" It was sound advice from years ago that had never rung more true.

Putting work first put "the company" in the driver's seat. Lizzie consistently rolled up her sleeves to fill the gaps at work. Over time, Lizzie had become a "one-stop shop" at work, accepting more responsibility without any regard for her wellbeing or self-worth.

Without realizing it, Lizzie had become the one person that others could count on to get the job done. They knew that she could be counted on to deal with things effectively, rationally and fairly, no matter how many hours in a week that it took. Although Lizzie was proud of her work and the relationships she had built over her career, her success had come at the ultimate cost.

After reading her SWOT, Lizzie knew she had to remove "the company" from the driver's seat, so that she could take the wheel and navigate her own journey. Lizzie could no longer be the "one stop shop." She had to put herself first, for once and for all.

Lizzie pondered her next steps. Would she leave a job she loved? Before she could make a decision about work, she needed more insights from her Four Wheels.

Lizzie had completed the first two steps. The

SWOT and flipping her limiting beliefs.

Passion was next. Lizzie knew it was important to be in the right environment to complete the Passion activity. The next beautiful, sunny day, Lizzie took another walk to think. When she got home, she chose to write in a sunny spot in her backyard gazebo. The fresh air, gorgeous view and cheerful birdsongs would surely inspire her. This is what she wrote:

Passion	
Your passions energize you and make you attractive to others. When you are clear about what moves you, you can seek out ways to link your passions with what you do and how you do it.	
Your Passion can be identified by answering the following questions:	
What would I do if money were not an issue?	I would volunteer for charities I believe in and offer free consulting and coaching services
I get really excited when...	When I help companies and people achieve growth and become their best selves, in work and in life
I love to...	Help others to see all the possibilities that life has to offer.

I live for…	My family and my faith.
I am here because…	I want to be a powerful force for good in the lives of others and in the world.

After completing these questions, you should see a common theme.

You might even want to highlight words that appear similar in your answers above.
Once you see a common theme, you have identified the thing you are most excited about - your passion.

Superpowers

Your superpowers are the things you do better than everyone else. Often, they are things you do with little effort. They are core to who you are. Some of us discount these strengths because we deliver these skills with little effort. Here are some questions to help you uncover your superpowers:

What do I do better than anyone else?	I am creative and caring. I use my creativity to think out of the box and come up with new ideas and trends that help people.

If I were to receive an award, what would it be for?	I'd like to think I'd be recognized for my spirit of giving back, freely and graciously.
What do others think I'm really good at?	Others see me as a confident leader who cares as much about people as about the success of the company.

You should see a commonality in your answers. Highlight the things that seem to be similar. These are your Superpowers.

Values

Your values are your guiding principles. They impact how you feel, behave and react. When you're living in alignment with your most important values, you are energized, confident and available to others. When you aren't, you create a drag on your energy.

The first step in aligning your values is knowing what they are and what gets in the way of being able to live in full alignment with them. Here are some questions to help you define your values:

What, in life is most important to me?	Faith, my family and making a positive impact in the world––I want to leave the world in a better place
What 3 things do I believe in more than anything else?	○ Everyone has the ability to do great things ○ Everyone wakes up each day wanting to do their best work ○ It takes one small act of kindness to change everything
What are my 3 biggest pet peeves?	○ People who are disingenuous, deceitful and stir the pot ○ People who disrespect others by their words and/or actions ○ Seeing anyone needlessly suffer

What situation makes me feel angriest or most annoyed?	When I don't keep my promises and let my family down.

As you review your answers above, you should see that your pet peeves, or the things that make you angriest or annoyed, are directly opposite to the things that are most important to you. Knowing both sides (your passion and your irritants) will give you clarity and help you to know if you have truly identified your values at the highest level. Your highest priorities.

Highlight any common themes in your answers.

Purpose

Your purpose is connected to how you want to contribute to the world beyond your career. It describes your role in turning your vision for humanity into reality. Having a purpose helps you identify what to pursue and what to avoid. Here are some questions to help you understand your purpose:

What's your biggest hope or dream?	To leave a legacy of positive impact in the lives of my children and in the world.

If you won the lottery, and didn't "need" to work, how would you spend your time?	Volunteering for charities Consulting for small companies free of charge Business and life coaching free of charge

Your answers should be similar in nature and one should support the other to help you know that you are on the right path.

Differentiation

Personal Brand is about standing out. If what you offer is the same as everyone else who does what you do, you are a commodity, not an irreplaceable brand. Understand and live your differentiation so you can attract the attention of those who are making decision about you.

Here are some questions that will help you get clear about what makes you unique:

What aspect of the world would be different if you had not been part of it?	Those I have coached over the years who have told me that I made a difference in the lives of their families perhaps would not have made the changes they did
What most strongly sets you apart from your peers?	My integrity

Knowing what makes you unique in the world will help you to fuel your passion and build your brand

How Others See You

The way that others see you is important in defining your brand because it's what they will first think of when someone says your name. If you are truly connecting with others using your highest priorities (those answers above) then others should clearly see you as you want to be seem.

Here is a question that will help you to see how others see you:

What do I think people say about me when my name comes up and I am not in the room?	I have a big work ethic and even bigger heart

When you review the answers above, and you don't think others see you as you want to be seen then you have some work to do.

Taking Stock

Lizzie compiled her answers as follows:

Carry your answers above to the grid below	
I identified my passion to be:	Helping others/Family
My superpower is:	Creative, out of the box thinker
My core values are:	Faith, my family and making a positive impact in the world
My purpose is:	To leave a legacy of positive impact in the lives of my children and in the world.
What sets me apart from others?	My integrity
Others see me as:	I have a big work ethic and even bigger heart I am strong yet humble

In working through the Passion activity, it was clear to Lizzie that she wasn't happy because she didn't have the time and energy to do the things that used to bring her joy.

She certainly wasn't living for her family. Her career had taken over her life, moving her in a direction that was less about pursuing her passion and working to her skill set and more about fixing problems. She was rolling up her sleeves to fill gaps and filling the cups of others while her own was running dry.

After looking through her journal, Lizzie was reminded of her Four Wheels journey and the questions she had hoped to answer:

Would she have a candid conversation with her boss? Would she leave a job she loved?

If Lizzie left, what would she do?

Was Lizzie even open to making the changes she needed to make herself? And even if she was open, did she have everything she needed in place to actually change?

From her coaching, Lizzie knew that, whenever someone contemplates change, they need to consider if they have everything they need to make the change relative to their skill and their mindset.

Lizzie reviewed the skill/mindset characteristics once more.

Mindset	Characteristics	What to do
The Expert	Stops themselves from doing something because they "aren't good at it" Driven by fear of failure which stems from self-limiting belief Self-limiting prophecy You will never become the expert unless you try	If you are the Expert, you want to take the time to evaluate and determine which limiting belief is holding you back. Then you can be begin to see things from a different perspective.
The Status Quo	Will tell you all the reasons why things shouldn't change Afraid of change Struggle with fear of failure	If you are The Status Quos you want to work through your fear of change by understanding and reframing your self-limiting beliefs to make a step in a positive direction.

The Procrastinator	Say they really "want" to learn but "something" is always in their way Will do almost anything or come up with any excuse to avoid doing something new Are people pleasers who take on too much or are plagued with self-limiting beliefs	If you are the Procrastinator, you want to focus on the real root issue of your procrastination to be able to make progress toward your goal.
The Armchair Quarterback	Ego focused Difficult to coach Says things like "I tried that and it doesn't work, or management doesn't understand" Look for sympathetic ears to rally the troops to their cause	If you are the Armchair Quarterback, you want to reframe your perspective by creating a pro and con value checklist and work through the list with an accountability partner or mentor.

The Ready, Willing and Able	Self-Aware Can easily articulate skills where they fall short Have emotional maturity Understand their areas of opportunity Open to evaluation and feedback	If you are The Ready, Willing and Able you are prime to learn and grow.

This activity should be easy, she thought. Lizzie had always considered herself to be of The Ready, Willing and Able mindset. After reviewing the characteristics, she could easily check the boxes:

Self-Aware	✓
Can easily articulate skills where they fall short	✓
Have emotional maturity	✓
Understand their areas of opportunity	✓
Open to evaluation and feedback	✓

Lizzie also knew deep down she had a bit of The Expert in her. She took pride in being good at things and could think of a few instances where she took the easy, comfortable path instead of taking something on because it "might" be a struggle.

This made sense. As someone with The Ready, Willing and Able mindset, Lizzie was able to see her areas of opportunity in another mindset. And she knew from experience that, while mindset characteristics overlap at times, your predominant mindset will guide you and help you work on other areas.

Reflecting on the work she'd done over the past week, Lizzie knew it was time to act. Moving forward in her journey meant engaging the Four Wheels and using her will to actually putting things into action.

But where would she go?

She couldn't stay put, overworked and unhappy. Something had to change. Lizzie also knew the company had a Status Quo mindset. So many times, over the past year when Lizzie pressed them to fill the gaps with a new hire, they put off making changes because the work was getting done.

Lizzie didn't begrudge the company she loved for being hesitant to make a change. She knew that change was difficult. She knew that Status Quo was a much easier path for most, and that human nature often chooses the path of least resistance.

That said, Lizzie had decided she needed to move away from Status Quo.

Lizzie had her answer: Move on.

While Lizzie valued the relationships with her colleagues and loved the role she had been hired for, her job had evolved into something that was no longer the right path for her. Big changes require bold moves and this was her moment. This was her time to put herself first, for the first time in years.

A few weeks later, Lizzie took the leap and left the company. This choice gave her the freedom to think about her next move, enjoy long overdue family time and even make some bucket-list memories.

Through it all, Lizzie never lost sight of the words she wrote that sleepless night, "I am not on the right path. I need help. I need to find my path and myself again." They were the jumpstart her Four Wheels journey needed, the words that got Lizzie back on the road in an energizing new direction. The sun was now behind her and her future looked wide open and inspiring.

Chapter 9
Hit the Road

Ups and downs. Ebbs and flows. On the road of life, they're inevitable. But don't let them stop you.

Most people feel blindsided when things don't go their way. But what if you were to know that there is a very real shift of emotions that comes with attempting anything you set out to do? Just like the gear shift on a car, you will shift through emotions that can blindside you if you aren't prepared.

Everyone experiences parts of these emotions, no matter who they are or where they are in life. While some may only experience one or two areas of the shift, others may run the full gamut of emotions. The point is, we can't turn off our emotions, so we need to lean into them.

Gear Shift of Emotions

When we set out to do something, we are *excited*. It's new! And we have high hopes and big goals to motivate us. Think about how excited you were to begin a new job or set a new goal. Think about how excited you were to open the first page of this book!

Over time, we can become *frustrated*. With frustration, we begin to experience challenges. We feel exasperated, defeated, even overwhelmed. Perhaps our new job was more difficult than we thought it would be or we didn't meet the first step of our goal.

Next, *self-doubt* creeps in. We lose confidence. We start to place blame. "If only I had been trained by Emma, I wouldn't be having the issues I am having." "If I had help from Laura in setting my goals, I would be knocking them out of the ball park." We may look for reasons to quit and say things like, "This isn't the job for me." "I need to do something else." "I have so much on my plate right now that I should take a break." "My children need me, so now isn't the best time." Or we begin to question ourselves: "Why I really doing this? I mean no one in my family supports me, so why am I really doing this?"

Next up is *procrastination*. We would do anything rather than do what we set out to do. We start coming in late to work. We spend too much time talking to others in the hallway. We clean or organize our office rather than working to hit our goals. We find reasons not to be successful and say things like, "You know this wasn't my strong suit to begin with." "I am not a numbers person." "I am really too busy for this." We start to make excuses and give up.

And then at times something happens. Something big that helps us reconnect with what we are doing and we experience *recommitment*. Maybe it's a small victory or a catalyst of some kind. A moment where we decide to keep going. Perhaps we found a mistake on the job that saved the company money or we attended a conference and had an epiphany. We can't wait to feel it again. Once again, we begin to take action, this time with a whole new commitment and *excitement*.

And the gears of emotions start all over again. Just like driving, we can shift through them over and over, every day or even multiple times a day! And at other times, we can shift our gear in reverse and get stuck on one emotion like doubt or creative avoidance for a very long time.

Much of the time we can get past many of the sticking points on our gear shifter by reviewing the lessons we learned in this book. Using the tools in our tool box and re-evaluating our Belief, Passion, Skill and Will helps us identify our areas of opportunity. Then we can confidently shift through emotions and get back on the road to success.

No matter where your road takes you, remember that the Four Wheels are your roadmap.

EXCITEMENT
Hope, positive energy, motivated, BIG goals, people believing in you.
RECOMMIT
Attend an event, or earn a reward or have an epiphany

SELF-DOUBT
Lose confidence, place blame, "I can't do it", look for reasons to quit, "Why am I doing this?"

FRUSTRATION
Experience challenges exasperated, defeated, overwhelmed, didn't meet your goal.

PROCRASTINATION
Do more work of another kind (cleaning your house, busy work), Find reasons not to be successful "Too busy", Make excuses, give up on your goal.

RECOMMITMENT
Have an "aha" moment, remember the "Why", experience life changes, experience a small victory, catalyst of some kind. Some sort of moment where you decide to keep going. Can't wait to feel it, decide to do it. Take action and feel the excitement all over again!

Reverse
You're stuck or you are going backwards

1 3 5

H

2 4 R

Whether you need to remove yourself from a toxic situation like Grace, garner support from your family like Wendy, get a boost in belief like Hannah, take back your passion like Tami, break the status quo like Andy, learn to empower others like Carrie or take a leap of faith like Lizzie, you now have the road map to make it happen.

Like your North Star, The Four Wheels will always guide you.

Belief is the destination.

Passion is the mode of transportation.

Skill is your compass…your road rules.

Will is getting behind the wheel and starting your journey.

Just like the wheels on your car, when one is misaligned, it pulls you in a different direction. It takes you off your path. If you get a flat, you are going to have to re-group and change your action, just like changing a tire. And if you wake up one day and someone has stolen one of your wheels, you are going to have to get a new wheel and a new perspective in order to keep moving toward your destination.

Remember that throughout your journey, you have a navigator with you. Like a GPS, your navigator is there to help get you back on track when you need it. Whether your navigator is the person you identified in chapter three, one of the lessons you learned in this book, a tool in your tool box or the Four Wheels community that you joined in my coaching program, you have a support system.

You are not alone. I've been where you are.

In the beginning of this book, I shared that I needed to make a change. I had coached so many people over so many years to use the principles of Belief, Passion, Skill, and Will to make great changes in their lives. Yet I hadn't always followed my own advice.

I wrote the framework for this book more than 10 years ago, but only recently had the fortitude to finish it. I found myself writing a couple of sentences here and there, only to become distracted or exhausted or just plain paralyzed by my daily work schedule and family life that I couldn't find time to fit it in.

All through my coaching, I had countless requests to write a book. Yet it wasn't until someone had the courage to tell me to stop talking about it and put my money where my mouth was that I committed to the final chapters.

It got me thinking about my life's next chapter and how I could use the tools that I had given to others to change the direction of my own path.

Along the way, I found the courage to share my story. You might be surprised to know that Lizzie is me. And atop my bucket list was writing this very book.

In beginning my own Four Wheels journey, I walked the very walk you're about to take. The tools I knew worked for so many others were now working for me—it was a game changer that changed my destination. I am now behind the wheel of a new journey, one that opens up the road to helping others on an endless highway.

I got off the couch and out of my own way—and I challenge you to do the same.

Here's to being a powerful force in the lives of others and in the world. We've got this, together.

To your success!

—Lisa

Appendix
The Four Wheels Tool Box

Personal SWOT (Chapter 1) - 1.1

Take 30 to 45 minutes in a quiet place to complete your own personal SWOT.

Strengths	Weaknesses
(Things you do well, positive personality traits, achievements)	(Negative work habits or personality traits, things you avoid)
Opportunities	**Threats**
(Resources, tools, training or networking groups that you participate in; things you do for you/personal and professional growth)	(Obstacles, challenges or threats to your business or personal life)

If you struggle with completing the SWOT, think about what your family, friends or peers would say about you if asked.

A SWOT analysis is a tried-and-true method businesses use to identify internal strengths and weaknesses and external opportunities and threats. The assessment is included in any successful business or marketing plan because it provides critical information needed to create a strategic plan for growth.

This important exercise is also invaluable for you, in both personal goal setting and as a coach. A personal SWOT is a creative method of self-assessment to determine where you (or the person you are coaching) are and where you (or they) can go.

A SWOT can help you better understand how to play to your own strengths or the strengths of those you mentor, as well as manage weaknesses, uncover opportunities for growth and eliminate threats that could keep you (or them) from moving forward.

If you or your mentee struggle to complete the SWOT, consider asking people you (or they) know well and trust (a spouse, friend or coworker) to review the completed matrix and provide honest feedback.

As a coach, you will use the personal SWOT to match strengths with opportunities and take aggressive action in those areas. Or match weaknesses with threats to discover situations that should be avoided. You can also use the information to convert weaknesses into strengths and threats into opportunities, when possible.

The amount of introspection and reflection that you put into a personal SWOT will only make it more meaningful and impactful. You'll see just how instrumental this tool is in beginning a journey of any kind.

SWOT Analysis Strengths and Weaknesses

In reviewing any personal SWOT, look for strengths to balance weaknesses. What this means is that people with certain strengths typically have corresponding weaknesses. As you look at the things you noted on your SWOT, look closely at the strengths and weaknesses section to see how your strengths and weaknesses match up.

If you don't see the typical strength and weakness balance below, you will want to do some reflection to ensure that you are fully self-aware and not in denial.

Keep in mind there will always be anomalies to some of the characteristics on this chart. Not ALL people who are confident struggle with humility, but many do, so it is listed as a POSSIBLE corresponding weakness. Your past environment and background could change some of these results but they give you a good place to start your self-reflection.

Strength	Possible Corresponding Weakness
Confident	Humility
Generous	Gives to a fault
Cautious	Passive
Logical	Emotionally Insensitive
Results Oriented, Direct, Determined, Relentless, Change Oriented	Demanding, Insensitive
Organized	Bossy
Optimistic, Visionary	Ignore red flags, Forget details
Good Communicator	Talks too much
Flexible	Inconsistent, Messy

Passionate	Impulsive
Nurturing	Procrastinates
Consistent	Slow Moving
Great Listener	Need reassuring
Dependable	Resistant to change
Loyal, Keeps the peace	Overly Tolerant
Detail Oriented	Fails to see the big picture
Open	Gullible
Sensitive	Takes things personally
Process Driven	Doesn't worry about results
Accurate	Perfectionist
Task Oriented	Critical of others and self
Humble	Passive
Energetic	Exhausting to others
Independent	Not a team player
Imaginative	Unrealistic
Honest	Blunt
Natural Leader	Bossy
Kind	Unassertive
Creative	Get bored quickly
Adaptable	Lacks structure
Realistic	Cynical
Charming	Pushes own agenda
Curious	Scattered – aimless
Emotional	Illogical
Patient	Unproductive - procrastinator

In reviewing your SWOT answers, journal on the following self-reflection questions:

- "Where do I think my strengths and weaknesses come from?"
- "How are they affecting my relationships with others and my life in general?"
- "What can I do about this?"
- "What would I change?"
- "What is my plan of action?"

Sample SWOT Review: Sheryl

Strengths	Weaknesses
(Things you do well, positive personality traits, achievements)	(Negative work habits or personality traits, things you avoid)
Organized, true friend, nurturer, relentless, helper and creative, always strive to do my best! I always find a way to get things done.	*Some people have accused me of being bossy or self-centered.* *Since I have so much on my plate, I tend to wait until the last minute to get things done, which makes some people crazy.*
Opportunities	Threats
(Resources, tools, training or networking groups that you participate in; things you do for you/personal and professional growth)	(Obstacles, challenges or threats to your business or personal life)
I am in a women's networking group and I try to get to the gym twice a week. I also try to read a self-improvement book once a month.	*I have a full-time job at my husband's business. I am a caregiver to my mother, who is in assisted living. I see her once and sometimes twice a day.*

In reviewing Sheryl's SWOT, she lists her strengths as organized and relentless. The corresponding weaknesses on the master chart (1.2) are bossy, demanding, and insensitive. Sheryl admits that others have accused her of being bossy and self-centered (which could be construed as insensitive). Although she believes that her procrastination is due to having so much on her plate, she procrastinates because she is nurturing. Nurturers by nature can't say no, so they put more on their plates than they can handle. Sheryl's nurturing qualities cause her to procrastinate by putting too much on her plate. She does take time for herself by reading, working out and networking with others but she may have more time if she could find some balance in her daily workload.

Because Sheryl is a nurturer and procrastinator, she may find it difficult to work through these issues on her own. She would be best served in working with a coach who could give her a plan of action and accountability benchmarks.

Sample SWOT Review: Andy

Strengths	Weaknesses
(Things you do well, positive personality traits, achievements) *Creative* *Optimistic* *Honest* *Great listener* *Kind* *Energetic*	(Negative work habits or personality traits, things you avoid) *Follow-through* *Technical Skills*
Opportunities	**Threats**
(Resources, tools, training or networking groups that you participate in; things you do for you/personal and professional growth) *Book Club* *Church Council* *Local Gym* *Rebuild Cars*	(Obstacles, challenges or threats to your business or personal life) *Poor business decisions have me financially strapped*

Because Andy is creative, he gets bored quickly (corresponding weakness chart), so it makes sense that follow-through would be difficult for him. Creative people are typically not technical thinkers, so that makes sense. If I were coaching Andy, I would thoroughly explore some other possible weaknesses that he has not listed like:

○ Kind – Unassertive

- Energetic – Exhausting to others
- Great Listener – Needs reassuring

Andy does appear to be well-rounded in the type of things that he does for personal and professional growth. I would also explore his threats more deeply. As someone who has made poor business decisions, Andy may have other areas of opportunity to work through in coaching.

The Four Wheels Grid – Self Reflection

In addition to the activities in the book, the Four Wheels Grid gives you the opportunity to reflect upon your abilities through journaling to the questions for each wheel (Belief, Passion, Skill, and Will).

Belief	Passion

Do I truly believe in myself as a driving force:
 	
    ○ In my business?
    ○ In my family?
    ○ In the lives of others?
    ○ As someone who can get it done?
 	
Do I think Positively?
 	
    ○ Do I see myself as successful?
    ○ As a successful business owner?
    ○ Successful in my career?
    ○ Successful in my family life?
	○ What are my talents and gifts?
	○ What types of jobs, projects or hobbies do I love?
	○ What excites me?
	○ What can I spend hours dreaming about?
	○ What can I spend hours talking about?
	○ What can I spend hours reading about?

Skill	Will
What am I really good at? ○ Am I a good speaker or writer? (Communication) ○ Do I make friends easily? (Social) ○ Do I do what I say? (Responsible) ○ Do I cope with change well? (Adaptable) ○ Do I support others? (Team player) ○ Do I meet deadlines? (Self-motivated) ○ Do I inspire others? (Leadership)	○ Do I find it easy or difficult to make decisions? ○ Am I often paralyzed by day-to-day activities or do I march forward to my plan? ○ Do I tend to overthink things in my life and in my business or do I jump in? ○ Do I worry about what others will think of me if I take a certain path or do I listen to my instincts? ○ Do I second guess myself and abandon a project, job or activity if things don't quickly work out or do I use my missteps to learn and move on? ○ Do I tend to fluctuate from thing to thing, project to project, or am I focused on the end game?

Journaling the answers to the questions and taking the time to reflect on your answers will not only help you to better understand your areas of opportunity but also help in conversations you might want to have with your navigator in setting goals or a family member in a family meeting.

Journal of Impact

You may not know it, but you have an incredible gift that you can readily and enthusiastically offer to others. You have a way of lighting the lives of others by offering them the gift of The Four Wheels: Belief, Passion, Skill, and Will.

When you live each day with purpose and on purpose, you show others their own unique value proposition in this world. You begin to clearly see your daily impact on the lives of others.

Start each day by journaling the following questions:
- "Who can I help today?"
- "In whose life can I make an impact today?"

End each day by journaling the following question:
- "Who did I help today?"

Daily reflection is powerful. When you do it consistently, can you imagine the pages you will write and the impact you will make on others and in the world?

What I love most about the Journal of Impact is that, when you have a bad day as we all do from time to time, you can look back and see the good you do. And in doing so, you can't help but be inspired—your seemingly bad day isn't so bad at all.

This is a servant mindset at its best. And it gives you clarity about why you do what you do and why you love what you do. As you look back over pages and pages of people you have helped—not for bragging rights but to see the good you do—you will feel the pride of serving others and be happy to continue this journey.

You'll feel really good having made an impact.

The Belief Grid

Think of a time when you should have taken a step but didn't:	
(A time when you really wanted to put something into action but fell short.)	
In childhood (Examples: reached out to a friend, auditioned for a play, stood up to a bully, stood up for a friend, etc.)	
In adult life (went for a promotion, met a new friend, took a risk, stood up for family or a friend, etc.)	
What stopped you from taking the step?	
In childhood	
In adult life	
What holds me back from achieving what it is I want? What are the barriers in my way?	
Why am I here? (In this world or in this business)	
In thinking of my life today, what is it that I want more of?	
(If I knew I could not fail and all barriers were removed, what would my life or business look like?):	

This month?	
This year?	
In five years?	
What limiting beliefs do I tell myself? (In all aspects of my life – business and personal):	
Do I use daily positive affirmations? Why or why not?	
If I could change one thing tomorrow, what would it be?	
Do I believe I am someone who is worthy and who can have all they want in life? Why or why not?	

The Passion Grid

Your passions energize you and make you attractive to others. When you are clear about what moves you, you can seek out ways to link your passions with what you do and how you do it. Your Passion can be identified by answering the following questions:	
What would I do if money were not an issue?	
I get really excited when…	
I love to…	
I live for…	
I am here because…	
After completing these questions, you should see a common theme. You might even want to highlight words that appear similar in your answers above. Once you see a common theme, you have identified the thing you are most excited about—this is your passion.	
Superpowers	
Your superpowers are the things you do better than everyone else. Often, they are things you do with little effort. They are core to who you are. Some of us discount these strengths because we deliver these skills with ease. Here are some questions to help you uncover your superpowers:	
What do I do better than anyone else?	
If I were to receive an award, what would it be for?	

What do others think I'm really good at?	

You should see a commonality in your answers. Highlight the things that seem to be similar. These are your Superpowers.

Values

Your values are your guiding principles. They impact how you feel, behave and react. When you're living in alignment with your most important values, you are energized, confident and available to others. When you aren't, you create a drag on your energy.

The first step in aligning your values is knowing what they are and what gets in the way of being able to live in full alignment with them. Here are some questions to help you define your values:

What is most important to me?	
What three things do I believe in more than anything else?	
What are my three biggest pet peeves?	
What situation makes me feel angriest or most annoyed?	

As you review your answers above, you should see that your pet peeves, or the things that make you angriest or annoyed, are directly opposite to the things that are most important to you.

Knowing both sides (your passion and your irritants) will give you clarity and help you know if you have truly identified your values at the highest level—these are your highest priorities.

Highlight any common themes in your answers.

Purpose
Your purpose is connected to how you want to contribute to the world beyond your career. It describes your role in turning your vision for humanity into reality. Having a purpose helps you identify what to pursue and what to avoid. Here are some questions to help you understand your purpose:

What's your biggest hope or dream?	
If you won the lottery and didn't need to work, how would you spend your time?	

Your answers should be similar in nature and one should support the other to help you know that you are on the right path.
Differentiation

Personal brand is about standing out.

If what you offer is the same as everyone else who does what you do, you are a commodity, not an irreplaceable brand. Understand and live your differentiation, so you can attract the attention of those who are making decision about you.

Here are some questions that will help you get clear about what makes you unique:

What aspect of the world would be different if you had not been part of it?	
What most strongly sets you apart from your peers?	

Knowing what makes you unique in the world will help you to fuel your passion and build your brand

How Others See You

The way others see you is important in defining your personal brand because it's what they will first think of when someone says your name.

If you are truly connecting with others using your highest priorities (those answers above), then others should clearly see you as you want to be seen.

Here is a question that will help you to see how others see you:

What do I think people say about me when my name comes up and I am not in the room?	

> When you review the answers above, and you don't think others see you as you want to be seen, then you have some work to do.

Taking Stock

Finally, compile your answers:

Carry down your answers above to the grid below	
I identified my passion to be:	
My superpower is:	
My core values are:	
My purpose is:	
What sets me apart from others?	
Others see me as:	

Review

Take some time to review your compiled answers. You should see an underlying commonality in your answers.

As you reflect upon your answers, how can you use the answers above to:

- Identify and fuel your passion?
- Create your personal brand?
- Strengthen your personal brand?
- Connect to others on a deeper level?
- Bridge your passion and personal brand with your company's brand, mission and core values?
- Make a memorable impact on those you meet?

- When they think of someone who can help them, someone they trust and connect with, they will think of you first.
- How can you bridge these answers to your business in an authentic way?

Family Board of Directors Meeting

Monthly Family Board Meeting Agenda *Meeting #1*	
Good News!	Everyone Shares
Set Goals	What is the big goal?
Define Roles and Responsibilities	Who is doing what?
Define Rewards	What's in it for each of us?
Inspirational Close	Congratulate and leave on a positive note

Monthly Family Board Meeting Agenda *Meeting #2*	
Good News!	Everyone Shares
Review Goals	How did we do?
Check in	Do we need to adjust or make changes anywhere?
Inspirational Close	Congratulate and leave on a positive note

Sample Business Goals Board

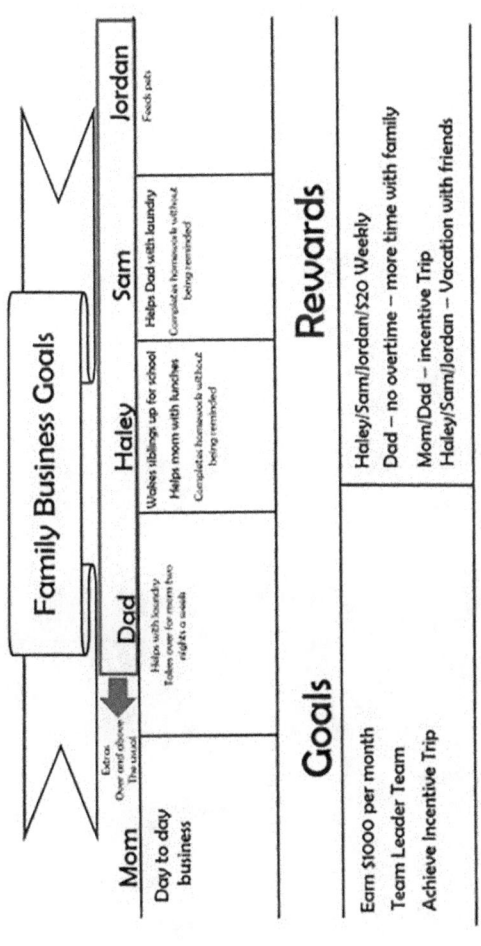

Lisa Hendrickson

To join the Four Wheels Community or to inquire about individual or group coaching:

lisa@fourwheelscoaching.com

Fourwheelscoaching.com